MINI-TALKS

Compiled by

Albert L. Zobell, Jr.

BOOKCRAFT INC.
SALT LAKE CITY, UTAH
1969

LITHOGRAPHED IN U.S.A. BY

PUBLISHERS PRESS
SALT LAKE CITY · UTAH

COMPILER'S PREFACE

Mini-Talks is another part of the Storyteller's Series.* We sincerely hope that as you prepare your presentations this book will do its bit to add zest to your thinking.

—*Albert L. Zobell, Jr.*

*Titles in the Series are: *Storyteller's Scrapbook, Storyettes, Story Gems, Story Sermons, Story Classics, Story Quotes, Story Lore, Story Beacons, Story Wisdom, Sermon Seedlings, Thoughts for Talks, Keys to Wisdom, Modern Parables, Quills of Truth, Topic Echoes, Notes to Quote, Talk Capsules, You, Too Remember . . . ,* and *File Favorites.* Earlier titles were *Minute Sermons* and *Sunlight and Shadows.*

Enoch challenged his city:

"Choose ye this day, to serve the Lord God who made you."

And together they made a heaven on earth.

CONTENTS

Contents

ACCOMPLISHMENT

The power of accomplishment is often a hair-line between success and failure. In fact, we are often able to do a task because we think we are able to do it.

———————

Josiah Quincy, one-time mayor of Boston and president of Harvard University, recalled:

"I will repeat an anecdote which I think Daniel Webster gave at a dinner, though, as I made no note of it, it is just possible that he told it in my presence at some later date. The conversation was running upon the importance of doing small things thoroughly and with the full measure of one's ability. This Webster illustrated by an account of some petty insurance case that was brought to him when a young lawyer in Portsmouth. Only a small amount was involved, and a twenty-dollar fee was all that was promised.

"He saw that, to do his clients full justice, a journey to Boston, to consult the law library, would be desirable. He would be out of pocket by such an expedition, and for his time he would receive no adequate compensation. After a little hesitation he determined to do his very best, cost what it might. He accordingly went to Boston, looked up the authorities, and gained the case.

"Years after this, Webster, then famous, was passing through New York City. An important insurance case was to be tried the day after his arrival, and one of the counsel had been suddenly taken ill. Money was no object, and Webster was begged to name his terms and conduct the case.

" 'I told them,' said Mr. Webster, 'that it was preposterous to prepare a legal argument at a few hours' notice. They insisted, however, that I should look at the papers; and this after some demur, I consented to do. Well, it was my old twenty-dollar case over again, and as I never forget anything, I had all the authorities at my fingers' ends. The Court knew that I had no time to prepare, and was astonished at the range of my acquirements. So, you see, I was handsomely paid both in fame and money for that journey to Boston; and the moral is that good work is rewarded in the end, though, to be sure, one's self-approval should be enough.' "

—————

You may have great plans and may be impatient to carry them out now. Possibly you can. We usually can do far more than we have believed. But possibly the best time has not arrived and the best place selected. Then be patient while you persevere. Great things require time, and the important projects must pass through many stages. However, if you are determined to accomplish what you have in mind, and do your utmost as well as give yourself the required time, you will certainly do it. All things come to him who waits patiently while he works efficiently.

ACTIVITY

My experience of nearly fifty years in the Church teaches me that I am either advancing toward my Father and toward his salvation, or I am retracing the steps that I have made. I am not standing still. There is no such thing in this Church. We are either in the light or in the darkness. When the sun sets in the west, gradually darkness steals upon us from the east until we are enveloped with it. The sun has not deserted the earth; but it has gone from us. While it is setting to us it is rising to somebody in another part of the earth. But when our minds become dark, how great is that darkness!

I have seen darkness steal over the minds of persons, and yet some of them will say they never

felt better in the Church in their lives. Look at the
life of such an individual. I said to him, "You
never felt better in your life in the Church?"

"No."

"Do you pay your tithing, brother?"

"Oh, no, I have stopped that."

"Do you pray with your family?"

"No, I do not pray with my family."

"Do you attend to your secret prayers?"

"No."

"And you never felt better in your life?"

"No, never felt better."

"Now, I know from my experience that a man
cannot feel well in the gospel unless he attends to
these things. How do you feel toward the Presi-
dency of the Church? How do you feel towards
the Twelve? How do you feel toward the presiden-
cy of the stake? How do you feel toward your
bishop? How do you feel toward your home
teachers? How are you toward your neighbor?"

"Well, I don't consider anybody around here fit to associate with, and really I am not comfortable in the presence of the president of the stake."

"What is the matter? Do you differ with him?"

"Yes, he doesn't preach the right kind of doctrine to suit me—but I never felt better in the Church in my life."

Now, as strange as it may seem, a man said that to me at one time. That man told me he was not doing the things I have mentioned, and yet he said he never felt better in his life. Is that encouraging the Spirit of God in his heart that will justify him before his Maker? I say no; he will never be justified by the Spirit of God while he lives in that darkness that he has seemed to allow himself to have entered. I know the spirit by which he said he never felt better in his life. I have seen it; and it is a snare and a delusion.

—President Brigham Young, Jr.

———

Use me, oh Lord:
Let not this day's declining sun,
Behold one duty still undone;
Nor let me falter by the way,
However great the heat of day.

Use me, oh Lord:
Thy willing servant I would be,
Subject in all things unto Thee;
And though my light may faintly gleam,
It may some errant soul redeem.

Use me, oh Lord:
For I am still a child of Thine,
Fashioned by hands that are divine;
I am a part, however crude,
Of Thy sublime infinitude.

Use me, oh Lord:
Let me not useless here abide,
A child to idleness allied,
Subject to sin's corroding power,
That blights the joy of every hour.

Use me, oh Lord:
Thou dost the twinkling stars so high,
The lofty peaks and hills near by,
And e'en the tiny drops of dew;
Oh Lord, in mercy, use me too.

Use me, oh Lord:
Why should I longer here remain,
If unto Thee I yield no gain?
If round my path the cobwebs loom,
Where only sweetest flow'rs should bloom?

Use me, oh Lord:
Stretch forth Thy guiding hand to me,
And lead me nearer unto Thee;
That in Thy service I may trace
The glory of my resting place.

—Hyacinth

———

AGE

A wise man will never rust out. As long as he can move or breathe he will be doing for himself, his neighbor, or for posterity. Almost to the last hour of his life Washington was at work; so was Newton. The vigor of their lives never decayed. No rust marred their spirits. It is a foolish idea to suppose that we must lie down and die because we are old. Who is old? Not the man of energy, not the laborer in science, art, or benevolence; but he only who suffers his energies to waste away and the springs of life to become motionless, on whose hands the hours draw heavily, and to whom all things wear the garb of gloom. Is he old? should not be asked, but is he active? Can he breathe freely and move with agility? There are scores of grayheaded men whom we should prefer in any important enterprise to those young men who fear and tremble at approaching shadows, and turn pale at a lion in their path, or a harsh word or a frown.

A good old age has learned to emphasize important things. It is sad to see one grown old only in years, or tall only in inches. Too many old men take delight in parade and show and externals, "childish things," not yet put away. A good old age emphasizes the abiding things.

A good old age becomes mellow and ripe. There is less of irritability, more of contentment. Children are a joy to a good old age. God is nearer.

But all old people are not good. Some are reaping the harvest of iniquity. The passions have never been chained. Jealousy and hatred have grown stronger with the decling years, when old age is a season of lamentations. Past memories rise up to shake their bony fingers and mock. Life goes out in the midst of clouds and lightnings.

But a good old age—one like a "slow drooping, mellow autumn after a rich and glorious summer"—an old age as beautiful as some of the glorious days, when the sun rises in the early morn, sheds its light in brightness and warmth throughout the day and at night drops out of sight, looking even larger before it disappears.

There is another kind of a good old age, still more beautiful, when the life has been hard and rough and thorny; it is the life of the great and good ones of the earth, the life of the true follower of our Lord and Master.

What is old age good for? No sadder sight on earth than to see one come to the last days, fruitless—when a harvest is expected. The summer ended, the autumn here and yet no reaper's songs of joy. No more glorious sight on earth or in heaven is there than to see the veteran, having finished his work, fought his fight, with the light of the future crowning, shining upon him!

A Christian old age is the best thing in the world.

—Reverend Sidney Strong

APPEARANCES

Once upon a time a cat who prided herself on her wit and wisdom was prowling about the barn in search of food and saw a tail protruding from a hole.

"There is the conclusion of a rat," she said.

Then she crept stealthily toward it until within striking distance, when she made a jump and reached it with her claws. Alas! it was not the appendage of a rat, but the tail of a snake, who immediately turned and gave her a mortal bite.

And if such a story has a moral, it surely must be that it is indeed dangerous to jump at conclusions.

———

As is gloriously sung in the Gilbert and Sullivan operetta "H.M.S. Pinafore," in the words of W. S. Gilbert:

> "Things are seldom as they seem,
> Skim milk masquerades as cream."

———

ATTITUDE

Although at the moment they may be equal in their lack of a real answer, the man who replies

"I'll find out," is much more valuable to his employer, his neighbor, and to himself than the man who replies "I don't know."

———

On a gloomy, rainy morning, it came little eight-year-old Tommy's turn to say the blessing at breakfast.

"We thank Thee for this beautiful day," he prayed.

His mother asked him why he said that when the day was anything but beautiful.

"Mother," said he, with rare wisdom, "never judge a day by its weather."

———

Like Satan himself, the lazy may quote scripture as an excuse for his condition. I have in mind one such selfish scriptorian. During a certain summer I had occasion to pass his farm almost daily. There were three trees on the place. If I failed to find him slumbering under the first, I was pretty sure to find him under one of the other two, any day. When once I inquired why he didn't cultivate his farm, and build something better than the log cabin in which his family lived in squalor, he reverently turned his eyes toward heaven and misquoted: "Blessed are the poor!"

Be it remembered that there are different kinds of poor. The poor are to be classified according to their merits and desserts. One of our local philosophers has presented a simple and comprehensive classification; he says there are three classes of poor people: (1) the Lord's poor; (2) the devil's poor; (3) the poor devils. If we be poor, let us belong to the worthy and respectable class of the poor.

—Elder James E. Talmage

BAPTISM

Baptism is only one of the rounds in the gospel ladder which reaches from the depth of the degradation into which poor humanity has fallen to the celestial kingdom. But the poor prisoner who wishes to escape from his dungeon must take step after step up the ladder until he reaches the top and can breathe once more the free air of heaven, or he will not be benefitted. The gospel is our means of gaining salvation. But we must obey

every principle or we cannot be saved; we must
take every step up the ladder, or we cannot get
into the celestial kingdom.

—President George Q. Cannon

———————

Earth's noon arrived! The Savior came!
And was by John of ancient fame
Baptized in Jordan's sacred tide,
A righteous law to thus abide—
Example setting to all men
How they must all be born again;
Born of water—people hear it!—
If God's kingdom they'd inherit.

—From "The Gospel Pioneer"
by Elder William Jefferies

———————

I have been at the Protestants' meeting many a
time, and have followed up their protracted
meetings, and sought for religion; and when people
were converted to the faith of Protestantism, I
have seen the minister go to the water because
some wished to be baptized in the water, but not
because it was at all necessary.

One would say, "I want to be sprinkled"; another, "I want to have the water poured upon me"; and another, "I want to be plunged."

"All right," said the minister, "either of these is just as necessary as the other, for none of them are essential to salvation; we only attend to them to satisfy the candidate."

Suppose the laws of the United States were made upon this principle, just to suit everybody's fancy and notions, making laws for everyone to do just as he pleased—what kind of laws would they be? What would you think of such a law-making department? Would you sustain it? Would you send to it a man, as a delegate, to represent your case, to make wholesome laws that would give every man his rights and privileges? I would not have such a law, but I would cast it out with those who made it.

—President Heber C. Kimball

BIBLE

If you have the "blues," read the twenty-seventh Psalm.

If your pocket book is empty, read the thirty-seventh Psalm.

If people seem unkind, read the fifteenth chapter of John.

If you are "all out of sorts," read the twelfth chapter of Hebrews.

If you are losing confidence in men, read the thirteenth chapter of First Corinthians.

If you can't have your own way in everything, read the third chapter of James.

———

Prosperity is the blessing of the Old Testament; Adversity is the blessing of the New.

—Francis Bacon

———

Get at the root of things: The gold mines of the scriptures are not the topsoil; you must open a shaft. The precious diamonds of experience are not picked up in the roadway; their secret places are far down. Get down into the vitality, the

solidity, the veracity, the divinity of the Word of
God, and seek to possess with it the inward work
of the Spirit.

———————

BLESSINGS

Isn't it strange that many of our greatest
blessings must come to us in disguise?

———————

Blessings star forth forever; but a curse
Is like a cloud—it passes.

—Philip J. Bailey

———————

BOOK OF MORMON

[This testimony was given by President Heber
J. Grant speaking at the Institute of Human
Relations, held at Estes Park, Colorado, August
10, 1936. Now, years later, with the marvels of
electronics, archeology, and other sciences that
bless mankind, we wonder what this Church
President would say.]

In my youth I was ridiculed for believing in the Book of Mormon because it says that the people of which it gives a record built houses of cement, and no cement dwellings had been found. I said, "Some day cement dwellings will be found, if not during my lifetime, when my children, grandchildren, or great-grandchildren come along."

The man said: "What is the use of talking with such a fool, who has to turn a knock-down argument over to his great-grandchildren. I will give you one you cannot possibly gainsay or turn over to others. That book teaches that Jesus Christ, after his resurrection, came to this continent and established his Church and he spoke to the people and his voice was heard all over the land. Now you know, youngster, that if you get up on top of a house and shout at the top of your voice, your voice will go only a few hundred feet, so you know that is a lie."

I said: "I do not know any such thing. I know that Jesus Christ, under God's command, took the elements existing and established this world, and I believe beyond question of doubt that if he wanted his voice to go all over the world he could have it do so at one and the same time."

Cement houses have been found in Mexico. A monument there covered with cement on the outside, which is 150 percent higher than the Mormon Tabernacle and covers eleven acres of ground, has been uncovered. From the top of that monument can be seen little mounds, and as they are uncovered by the United States and Mexico, they are found to be very splendidly built cement houses with drainpipes of cement, showing a skill in the use of that material the equal of anything in our day.

"The fool," according to the man with whom I had the discussion, has sat in his home with a little box in the corner and listened to Admiral Byrd talking from the South Pole. All my life I have been finding additional evidences that the Bible is the book of books and that the Book of Mormon is the greatest witness for the truth of the Bible that has ever been published.

———

I had a conversation with a would-be censor of our sacred books. He accosted me on the street with the question: "Bishop Whitney,* do you believe the Book of Mormon to be the word of God?"

"I certainly do," said I.

"Well, can't God speak grammatically?"

"Of course he can."

"Then why was this grammatical error left in the Book of Mormon?" and he quoted it.

"Do you really want to know?"

"Yes," he said.

"Well, I think that was left there just to keep you out of the Church."

He seemed surprised: "Doesn't God want me in his Church?"

"No," I said; "He only wants honest seekers after truth; and, if you think more of a grammatical error than you do of your soul's salvation, you are not fit for the kingdom of heaven, and the Lord doesn't want you."

He was astonished. It was something he hadn't considered. He felt very much as Goliath did when the stone sank into his forehead—such a thing had never entered his head before.

—Elder Orson F. Whitney

*He was bishop of the Eighteenth Ward, Salt Lake City, at his call to the Apostleship, and carried the bishop title affectionately throughout life.

———

BROTHERHOOD

Some of the lessons, the impressive lessons, of my life have been taught in very simple ways, and this was one of them:

In my early life, in a limited way I was a freighter. The etiquette of the road required that a man going downhill should give the road to the man going uphill; or the man with the lighter load should give it to the man with the heavier load; but there were some men on the road who were possessed of the idea that no matter what the etiquette of the road demanded, the other fellow should always turn out.

I remember once a friend of mine driving along a freight road leading to Pioche, Nevada. He met a team with a young fellow driving it and they came up pretty close together.

Hank stopped his horses and said, "Are you going to get out of the road?"

"No," the boy replied, "I can't very well get out, where I am here."

"Well, you will have to get out," and one word brought on another until Hank climbed down off of the high seat of his wagon and started over to take it out of the boy's hide.

A little later some of us drove along and found him sitting there by the side of the creek washing the blood off of his face.

One of the boys said, "What is the matter, Hank?"

"Oh," he said, "nothing. I just made a mistake in judgment, that is all."

*****

Shortly after that I was again on the road. There was a man freighting there who always carried a gun on the spring seat with him, not a gun around his waist, but a double-barrel shotgun that he could use very quickly. He never was without it, and he was a terror wherever he went.

One day, when I was pulling up a grade, in the mud after a rainstorm, I saw the ears of his big mules flopping over the top of the hill, and when he came in sight about the first thing I noticed was the shotgun.

The etiquette of the road required him to turn out, and when our teams came close together, they stopped.

He looked at me through his grizzly beard and said, "Young man, are you going to get out and give me the road?"

I said, "I can't very well get out."

He said, "Do you know what I will do, if you don't?"

"No, sir," I said, "I don't know."

"Why," he said, "I will get out."

"Well," I said, "if you will just pull your mules' heads around a little, I will make my horses pull this load out of the road if they can.

We both turned out and each, giving part of the road, passed. Now, I have told you that simple story because it illustrates this thought: Which of the two men was the good neighbor; Which of the two men did the right thing?—the man who was determined that the other fellow should turn out and who made a mistake in judgment, or the man who might very easily have prevailed and dominated the road, who was willing himself to give half of it and be satisfied?

—President Anthony W. Ivins

CHILDREN

He hunted through the library
   He looked behind the door,
He searched where baby keeps his toys
   Upon the nursery floor.
He asked the cook and Mary,
   He called Mamma to look,
He even started sister up
   To leave her storybook.

He could not find it anywhere,
   And knew some horrid tramp
Had walked in through the open gate
   And stolen it, the scamp!
Perhaps the dog had taken it
   And hidden it away,
Or else perhaps he'd chewed it up
   And swallowed it in play.

And Mamma, coming down the stairs,
   Looked through the closet door.
And there it hung upon its peg
   As it had hung before.

And Tommy's face grew rosy red,
   Astonished was his face,
He couldn't find his cap—because
   'Twas in its proper place.

            —Emma Endicott Marran

A small daughter came to visit her father at his offices in the factory that the family owned.

"Come with me," the father said, opening the door to the factory work area.

"But Daddy, I don't want to—the noise—it all scares me so."

"Daughter," the man said gently, taking her by the hand, "do you not know that I am the master here?"

And with that he threw the master switch and immediately every wheel in the factory slowed to a stop and the noise subsided.

———

"Mom, you don't have to worry about me," said an eight-year-old boy, as he left for a friend's party. "All I do is behave like I want to come next time. And I do!"

———

CHRISTMAS

Christmas, to the Latter-day Saints, is both reminiscent and prophetic—a reminder of two great and solemn events, which will yet be regarded universally as the mightiest and most wonderful happenings in the history of the human race. These events were predestined to take place upon this planet before it was created. One of them was the coming of the Savior in the Meridian of Time, to die for the sins of the world; and the other is the prospective advent of the risen and glorified Redeemer, to reign upon the earth as King of kings.

> —The First Presidency in 1907
> [President Joseph F. Smith
> President John R. Winder
> President Anthon H. Lund]

The discussion turned to "The Christmas I Remember Best" and this was reverently recalled:

"Mine was a railroad family. Dad worked two days of three, which meant two Sundays of three, and two Christmases as well. Christmas came with the calendar, but it really started later that day, or the next day, when the train was in and we had met the streetcar. We learned early as children that the day could be made by the deed. It was a good life, not to be wished away for anything.

"After I had grown and was ordained an elder, we moved to another ward. My new quorum had the LDS Hospital assignment of administering to the sick night and morning each day of Christmas week. Understandably many of my quorum brothers with wives and small children would have preferred that activity at a different time of the year. But I always volunteered to be one of several elders to go on Christmas morning, realizing that visiting and administering to the sick that morning always brought a peace and joy with its sweet spirit.

"One Christmas Eve I received a telephone call. My quorum president said that an elder assigned for that evening had other responsibilities. Could I go in a few minutes as well as take my own assignment in the morning? I was ready. The assignment was filled, but I came home with shoes wet in the new fallen snow.

"My shoes were still wet Christmas morning. That delayed me only a moment. Dad was over three hundred miles away, but I knew where he kept his new shoes. I put them on and was off to the hospital again to administer to the sick.

*****

"Now I have a twelve-year-old son who is a deacon. He borrows my ties to wear on his Church assignments, and lately I have noticed that he has taken as his own a nice blue one that I thought I had put away for special occasions.

"I look at him with his broadening shoulders and growing feet and hope that he continues on the Lord's errands, and some time, perhaps on a Christmas morning, to meet his commitments he may borrow my shoes to see that the work of the Lord is accomplished."

————

We think tenderly, lovingly of the birth of the Christ-Child in Bethlehem's lowly manger, and as we contemplate the matchless life and how Jesus "led captivity captive and gave gifts unto men," we ask ourselves what can we do to be worthy of this Elder Brother, how can we show our appreciation for that which he has bequeathed to us? In answer to the query methinks I hear the voice of Christ saying, "Freely ye have received, freely give." Give what? Kind words, loving deeds, generous gifts? Yes, but more than all these we should give ourselves. We should enter the Father's service with all that we have and are.

Jesus came that we "might have life and have it more abundantly," and as joint heirs with him we should see that our neighbors have a bigger, fuller life because we live. Each life should be a benediction to those that come in contact with it.

If each would foster the divine spark that is within him and cause it to burst forth into flame, each would shed forth a light as he passes among his fellows which would be a beacon showing them the way.

When we give a gift we desire it to be beautiful and useful. Ere we give ourselves we should become beautiful by cleansing from sin; useful by acquiring knowledge and ability to serve in whatever field the Master may designate. Our talents must not be folded in napkins and laid away. They must be put where they will increase, bring interest, double themselves. Then will the Master give unto us other talents and we shall grow more worthy of our King.

CHURCH

Thomas J. Yates, a returned Southern States missionary, attended Cornell University, where in 1900 he attended a public reception honoring Dr. Andrew D. White, then United States Ambassador to Germany. Each student was personally introduced to Dr. White who had served for seventeen years as the first president of Cornell. Upon meeting Elder Yates he asked if he were a Mormon. Hearing an affirmative answer he asked this student to come to see him later.

During the promised interview later in Dr. White's study, the young man from Scipio, Utah, learned that Dr. White had served, in 1892, as U.S. Foreign Minister to Russia. There the American educator had become acquainted with Count Leo Tolstoi, the great Russian author, statesman, and philosopher. A warm friendship existed between the two men, who often discussed their views.

On one occasion, Dr. White found Count Tolstoi in the fields, saying: "I am very busy today, but if you wish to walk beside me while I am plowing, I shall be pleased to talk with you."

As the two men walked up and down the field, they discussed many subjects, among them religion.

"Dr. White," said the Count, "I wish you would tell me about your American religion."

"We have no state church in America," was the reply.

"I know that, but what about your American religion?"

Patiently then Dr. White explained that in America there are many religions, and each person is free to belong to his own choice of churches.

Then Tolstoi impatiently replied: "I know all of this, but I want to know about the *American* religion. Catholicism originated in Rome; the Episcopal Church originated in England; the Lutheran Church in Germany; but the Church to which I refer originated in America, and is commonly known as the Mormon Church. What can you tell me of the teachings of the Mormons?"

"I know very little concerning them," Dr. White admitted.

"Dr. White," the Count continued, "I am greatly surprised and disappointed that a man of your great learning and position should be so ignorant of this important subject. The Mormon people teach the American religion; their principles teach the people not only of heaven and its attendant glories, but how to live so that their social and economic relations with each other are placed on a sound basis. If the people follow the teaching of this Church, nothing can stop their progress—it will be limitless. There have been great movements started in the past but they have died out or been modified before they reached maturity. If Mormonism is able to endure, unmodified until it reaches the third and fourth generation, it is destined to become the greatest power the world has ever known."

———————

As I have looked over the congregation of Saints, no thought has impressed me more than that here we have all classes and all manner of people, unlike in their God-given gifts, are finding the satisfaction of their lives, after they have once accepted the gospel, in the doctrines and the life within the Church.

Whether of high or of low degree, rich or poor, learned or unlearned, of quick or of slow intelligence, from Scandinavia, Germany, England, or America, these people, because of the gospel and through the gospel, see alike, apparently think alike, and very largely act alike. There is something within this gospel that unifies all who accept it and who belong to it.

This is not true alone of this generation and of this dispensation. It has been so in all ages, in all generations, and in all dispensations. The Patriarch Enoch in his holy city, Abraham on the Plains of Mamre, Moses in the wilderness, Samuel in God's temple, and all the other worthies of which history gives an account, gained strength and found the solace of their lives in the identical gospel to which we adhere and to which we give our allegiance.

—Elder John A. Widtsoe

COMMANDMENTS

Along comes a man and says, "It is all folly to
have faith in the name of Jesus. It is true that
Christ died for all, but it is folly for you to fret
yourselves about keeping his commandments and
observing the ordinances left on record in the
scriptures. Jesus will save all. He did not come to
call the righteous, but sinners to repentance, and if
he came to save the sinners do you not think he
will accomplish the task?"

We, the Latter-day Saints, certainly believe that
Christ will accomplish all that he undertook to do,
but he never yet said he would save a sinner in his
sins, but that he would save him *from* his sins. He
has instituted laws and ordinances whereby this
can be effected.

But this gentleman says, "Christ will save all."
The Mormon elder says that he will save all who
come to him, all who hearken to his word and
keep his commandments, and Jesus has said, "If ye
love me, keep my commandments." Now this
character to which I have referred says he loves
Jesus, but it is nonsense to keep his commandments; but the "Mormon" says, "I love Jesus, and
in proof of it I keep his commandments."

Now, suppose the former is correct and Christ
will save all, whether they do or do not keep his

commandments, in that case the "Mormons" are right again, for they will all be saved; but suppose that Jesus requires strict obedience to his laws and ordinances and commandments, those who merely believe without rendering obedience to his laws are slightly incorrect, and, in the end, the disadvantage will again be with them.

—President Brigham Young

COMPROMISE

The fabled story of Aladdin and his magic lamp has an important lesson for the youth of the Church. You will recall that Aladdin esteemed his lamp as a thing of little value until he learned the secret of its great power. Then, another who knew of the amazing service rendered by the genie to the possessor of this lamp, sought by trickery to gain possession of it. The strategy the thief used was as old as man. He cried in the streets, "New lamps for old . . . new lamps for old."

Aladdin's wife, who saw only the old form of her husband's lamp, was attracted by the glitter and ornamentation of the new lamps offered by the trader in the street. Without knowing what she was doing, she gave away a possession of great value for a cheap thing, the worth of which began and ended with its outward appearance.

One does not wait long in life to be greeted by the call, "New lamps for old . . . give up what you have for something with more glamour." This is particularly true for members of the Church, who have something of greater worth than Aladdin's lamp, genie and all.

The call usually comes first from companions who tempt us to abandon standards we have been taught in our homes and in the Church. The arguments advanced to break down our resistance always include a charge that the standards are old-fashioned and they no longer are realistic in terms of the way the world lives today. Then, too, we are urged to "do as the group does." Individualism, as a definition of holding to personal ideals, is classed as obstinacy and anti-social. Inevitably we run point blank into the evils of compromise.

When compromise enters our moral fibre, it spreads like a cancerous growth. We think we plan adequate safeguards around areas in which we contemplate yielding our standards, but once we lower the fence and break our strong will to do right, come what may, we expose ourselves to forces that spread beyond control. Compromise always starts on some rather insignificant principle. The dangers of yielding seem negligible and we usually risk those things first where observation and detection by others is difficult. We thus seek to avoid censure and discipline. In a short time we find ourselves trading our principles for false values and doing it in the black market of human relationships. . . .

Ask to see the genie before you trade your old lamp!

—Elder Ralph W. Hardy

———

Compromise, like so many things, can be good or bad, depending upon its application. As James Russell Lowell once defined it:

"Compromise makes a good umbrella, but a poor roof; it is a temporary expedient, often wise in party politics, almost sure to be unwise in statesmanship."

———

CRITICISM

Always remember, no one can debase you but yourself. Slander, satire, falsehood, injustice—these can never rob you of your manhood. Men may lie about you, they may denounce you, they may cherish suspicions manifold, they may make your failings the target of their wit or cruelty. Never be alarmed; never swerve an inch from the line your judgment and conscience have marked out for you. They cannot, by all their efforts, take away your knowledge of yourself, the purity of your character, and the generosity of your nature. While these are left, you are unharmed.

———

The real aim of criticism is not the destruction of cherished traditions—although a due regard for the facts does often compel us to revise older opinions—but a fuller appreciation of the beauty and truth of the creative work on which it fixes its regard. The word "criticism" is derived from the Greek word *kritikos,* which means "the ability to select or discriminate," hence, to decide or judge. The meaning of criticism is thus discriminating judgment.

———

DEATH

Latter-day Saints in their preaching, call on men and women to prepare to live, and they teach them how to live, believing that if any person is prepared to live as he ought to, he will certainly be prepared to die whenever the summons shall come.

—President George A. Smith

—————

If we could know
Which of us, beloved, would be first to go,
Who would be first to break the swelling tide,
And step alone upon the other side—
    If we could know!

    If it were you,
Should I walk softly, keeping death in view?
Should I my love to you more oft express?
Or should I grieve you, beloved, any less—
    If it were you!

    If it were I,
Should I improve the moments slipping by!
Should I more closely follow God's great plan,
Be filled with sweeter charity to man—
    If it were I!

    If we could know!
We cannot, beloved, and 'tis better so.
I should forget, just as I do today,
And walk along the same old stumbling way—
    If I could know.

I would not know
Which of us, beloved, will be the first to go,
I only wish the space may not be long
Between the parting and the greeting song;
But when, or where, or how we're called to go—
I would not know.

—Anonymous

DUTY

According to the ancient Greeks, when Hercules was a boy, just reaching the period of life when there was a question in his mind which path he should pursue, he went forth by himself and sat down and meditated.

There came to him someone in the form of a beautiful young woman.

"Hercules, I know what you want," she said; "the path that I will point out to you will bring pleasure, will bring you constant place in society, will bring you the choice things of life, to eat and to drink and clothing to wear. You shall be popular in the society in which you shall move, and your whole life will be one constant round of pleasure."

"What is your name?" Hercules asked.

"My enemies call me Vice, but my friends call me Pleasure," she replied.

Then there appeared to him another beautiful woman and she said:

"Hercules, I shall not deceive you; the path I shall point out to you will be a path of labor, a path of toil, a path of self-sacrifice, a path in which you must devote a great deal of your effort and energy; you will have to forget yourself; you will have to serve your friends; you will have to serve the people of Greece; but if you will take this path and pursue it, although it may bring to you much toil and privation and many sacrifices, you shall become immortal."

Hercules asked: "What is your name?"

She replied: "My name is Duty."

————

The path of duty is the only path of safety. It is the only path wherein we can walk and have the assurance of God's continued blessings, of his continued deliverances. Any other course does not carry with it this assurance.

Any other path leads to darkness, to contention, to evils of many kinds; for it leads away from the truth and the right. But if we continue in the path that is marked out for us by divine instruction, trusting implicitly in God, then shall we be delivered from all impending evils that are sought to be brought upon us, no matter what they may be; and the nearer we live to God the greater will be the blessings showered upon us, and seeming evils will be changed to blessings of untold worth.

—President George Reynolds

EXAMPLE

This is an age-old truth: People seldom improve when they have no other model but themselves to copy.

If I desire my children to tell the truth, I must also tell the truth. If I desire them to be virtuous and honest, I must be virtuous and honest. If I desire them to be industrious, I must be industrious myself. If I desire them to honor God, I must honor him in my life. Whatever I desire my children to do, I ought to do it myself. Example is stronger teaching than all the precepts we can give our children.

—President Joseph F. Smith

FAILURE

One great source of failure is found in a lack of concentration of purpose. There will be adverse winds in every voyage, but the able seaman firmly resists their influence, while he takes advantage of every favorable breeze to speed him on his course.

So in our aims and pursuits we shall find much to counteract them, much to draw our attention from them, and, unless we are armed with a steadfast purpose, that can subordinate the lesser to the greater, that can repel hindrances, resist attractions, and bend circumstances to our will, our efforts will not be crowned with success.

> Keep pushing—'tis wiser
>   Than sitting aside,
> And dreaming and sighing,
>   And waiting the tide;
> In life's earnest battle
>   They only prevail

Who daily march onward
    And never say fail!

With an eye ever open
    A tongue that's not dumb,
And a heart that will never
    To sorrow succumb,
You'll battle and conquer
    Though thousands assail;
How strong and how mighty,
    Who never say fail!

The spirit of angels
    Is active I know
As higher and higher
    In glory they go;
Methinks on bright pinions
    From heaven they sail
To cheer and encourage
    Who never say fail!

In life's rosy morning,
    In manhood's firm pride,
Let this be your motto,
    Your footsteps to guide—
In storm and in sunshine,
    Whatever assail,
We'll onward and conquer
    And never say fail!

                    —Elder R. H. Stringfellow

Nothing is easier than fault-finding. No talent, no self-denial, no brains, no character are required to set up in the grumbling business. But those who are moved by a genuine desire to do good have little time for murmuring or complaining.

—Robert West

_____

FAITH

[Elder George A. Smith, then a member of the Council of the Twelve but later a counselor to President Brigham Young, went with Elder John Taylor to Washington, D.C., in 1856 to try to obtain statehood for the Territory of Utah. He reported this as he spoke at a general conference of the Church.]

"After my return home, some of the brethren asked me how much faith I had that we should be admitted. I concluded my faith had been like that of a certain pious lady, whose minister called upon her and inquired concerning her religious welfare. She replied that she was well satisfied with her spiritual progression, but in her temporal welfare she was not equally prosperous. She was destitute of bread and had nothing to sustain life.

"The minister kindly told her to exercise faith and she could make stones into bread. She thanked him for his timely advice, she had never thought of that, and accordingly went and procured some stones of suitable size for loaves of bread, washed them, put them into pans, heated her oven in which she placed them, closed the door, exclaimed, 'I have firm faith, that when these stones come out of the oven they will be good bread.'

"After patiently waiting the proper time, she opened the oven door and looked anxiously in; 'There!' she declared, 'they are stones yet, and I *knew* they *would be* all the time.' "

The Bible, or another book of scripture at my father's place at meal times, was the order of the day in the home of my youth. He would read a chapter aloud and lead the discussion.

But one day as we assembled for our meal, there was no book of scripture but a single watermelon seed. He appeared not to notice the omission but recalled something he had discussed concerning faith several days previously. We all joined in on the lively discussion.

Then tenderly, almost reverently, he picked up the watermelon seed and held it.

"Boys," he said, still studying the seed. "Do you believe that there is the possibility of several watermelons here in my hand?"

We all nodded in agreement.

"Do you believe that I have the beginnings of a whole wagon load of watermelons here?"

One of my older brothers said that he couldn't say that, but he'd like to plant the watermelon seed and see. We all agreed with my brother.

"Boys," Father said with a twinkle in his brown eyes, "you have the right idea. Prove your faith by your works."

—Elder A. L. Zobell (Sr.)

———————

A religious writer once gave a convincing illustration for the existence of Deity by showing that there is no such thing as chance, but that behind every object animate or inanimate there is a power that exercises the creative act; behind every design there is a designer, and behind every plan is a mind that planned.

He takes a watch for example. Thus: An infidel in passing through a field, discovered a peculiar object lying in his path, the like of which he had never seen before. He picked it up and found by close examination that it was a little piece of mechanism, marvelous in construction, with a variety of pins and wheels and springs arranged and combined with such consummate skill that, when set in motion, the time of the day, the hour and minute and second, was indicated. While the intricate mechanism itself commanded his admiration, he saw at a glance that the real purpose sought to be accomplished by this wonderful piece of workmanship was the marking of the time.

He carried it home and showed it to a friend, who, greatly admiring it, said, "Of course you will agree with me, that this curious piece of mechanism was not created or made, but simply came into the field by chance."

"No," replied the infidel, who had ever doggedly maintained there is no God, no Creator, "an intelligent mind conceived it and a skilled hand fashioned it."

There is undoubtedly a great creative power, or force, behind these mighty wonders of the heavens and the earth that are daily visible to the human eye, and that is the power of God.

———————

The late Nephi Jensen, one-time judge in Salt Lake City, once strolled as a mission president with a young elder in Canada. They looked at a new bridge spanning a great river and commented upon the engineering skill that was there.

The young missionary exclaimed, "Steel is the strongest thing in the world."

"No," the mission president quietly answered. "Faith in God is stronger than steel. On the bridge of our faith we can span space and go directly into the presence of our Father in heaven."

———————

FIRST PRINCIPLES

When I was preaching in Kentucky I preached upon the first principles of the gospel, and at the close of my discourse I gave the privilege for anyone to ask questions or to make remarks, if they felt so disposed.

A gentleman arose, and I noticed that a great many of the congregation began to laugh; and I afterwards learned that the gentleman was an infidel, and hence the congregation were disposed to make fun of him.

He said: "I will not detain you long but I wish to state to this large congregation that Mr. Woodruff has taught me more this evening than I ever learned in my whole life before. From my boyhood I have been searching into religion; and when I have asked a minister in relation to the way of life, he would point me to the way he was walking himself; then I would ask another, and he would point out a different way; and I might have asked a hundred, and they would all have pointed out a different road, and they would tell me that I must be born again.

"I observed men who were said to be born again, and one class of men who were said to be born again would take one way, and another would take quite a different road; and I always marveled at this, for I did not see any sense in men taking different roads to lead to the kingdom of heaven.

"But now, this man, Mr. Woodruff, has told me the truth, and shown me the reason they took so many different roads after they were born again; and the reason is, because they were all born *blind.*"

—President Wilford Woodruff

FIRST VISION

A minister said to me at one time that he thought we were too positive about the things of religion. He thought we had not considered the question of God enough to be able to speak with such certainty. He informed me that he belonged to a church that was several hundred years older than the one to which I belonged, and that his church had been considering these questions for a long time and had altered their view and their opinion about many theological questions.

I granted that that was true; and he ventured the assertion that after we had been discussing these theological questions as long as they had, perhaps we would change our opinion also. He used this illustration:

"If you had a problem and you selected ten boys to solve the problem, and you gave one of them ten days in which to study it, and another boy nine days and still another boy eight, and so forth, until you had one boy studying the problem but one day and one studying ten days; which boy, at the conclusion of his studies, would know most about the problem? The one who had been studying but one day or the one who had studied ten days?"

I had to concede, that if all things were equal, of course the boy that had been studying ten days ought to know most about the problem.

"There you are," he said; "we have been studying it longer than you have, and you are one of the youngest churches, and so you are likely to change your mind when you study it a little longer."

"But," I said, "suppose the boy who has had the problem but one day receives the visit of a professor who knows all about the problem and who illustrates it so that now it is prefectly clear to the mind of the boy, who knows most about it, the boy who has thus been aided, only having had the chance to study it one day, or the boy who has been dreaming about it for ten days?"

"Why," the minister said, "of course, the boy who was thus aided and assisted knew most about the problem."

Then I said: "That is exactly where we stand." And I bore my humble testimony that Joseph Smith did not know, because of earthly wisdom and his reading of the scriptures, more about our Father in heaven and his Son Jesus Christ, than the learned ministers of the world. Not by that means did he obtain his knowledge, but in the time he was in the Sacred Grove in the presence of the Father and the Son he knew more about God the Eternal Father and his Son Jesus Christ than all the ministers of all the world had ever known, or ever will know, except they shall be, in like manner, informed and instructed. The great wisdom that had come to him was from the source to which men must go if they shall know our Father in heaven.

—Elder Melvin J. Ballard

GENEALOGY

"Genealogy is certainly misnamed," lamented a good Church member, "the very name genealogy makes me think of rigor mortis, and I react accordingly by inactivity. But if it were called something like 'turning the heart of the children to the fathers,' which it certainly is, that's a very warm, and interesting, and fascinating activity."

"Behold, I will send you Elijah the prophet before the coming of the great and dreadful day of the Lord:

"And he shall turn the heart of the fathers to the children, and the heart of the children to their fathers, lest I come and smite the earth with a curse." (Malachi 4:5-6.)

That scripture is often quoted by speakers in behalf of genealogical effort in the Church.

But what of the other verses in Malachi's six-verse chapter? What do they mean? The first verse which reads:

"For behold, the day cometh, that shall burn as an oven; and all the proud, yea, and all that do wickedly shall be stubble: and the day that cometh shall burn them up, saith the Lord of hosts, that it shall leave them neither root nor branch."

Is it not logical that the phrase ". . . it shall leave them neither root nor branch" refers to the sealing together in the temples, which should be done, but in many cases isn't because people are not working in that endeavor?

———

GOALS

At a fork in the road in the early 1930's in northern Utah a family stopped for a meal.

"Where does the left fork go?" the waitress was asked.

"To Paradise—but it doesn't go through." She hesitated, then, "That doesn't sound right, does it? There's a small town at the end of the road, Paradise. But the road makes no connections for a traveler going anyplace else."

Over the years we've thought about that. All of us have the best intentions in the beginning of traveling to a heavenly goal. But how many of us are content when we find a road to our liking, knowing full well that it "doesn't go through" to our intended destination.

———

An elderly gentleman recalled once camping out hunting cattle with a group of men. One of the men had an extremely intelligent horse and the conversation turned to what that horse could do, and someone asked him if the horse could tell an unbranded calf, as some had said.

He replied: "No, that is just a joke, but when I start him after an animal he will never lose track of it."

Then beginning a story, he said: "I once went to Pioche with a bunch of beef. For reasons of my own I did not want to be seen coming back so my friend was to keep a fire on the Iron Mountain in order that I might cross the desert in the night. I left the mountain near Desert Spring at dark. It was about ten miles before we reached the flat of the desert where there were low places from which I could not see the fire for some time, that I would not be able to tell where to look for the fire.

"But when I went into a low flat where I could not see the light and then came on high ground where I could see it, the light of the fire was right between that horse's ears, so I knew that he knew that that fire was where we were going. He had learned that in the first ten miles. All night long I had no trouble about it. He would avoid obstacles and always come back to the line."

There are some who are, as the scriptures say, unstable, wafted about with every wind of doctrine. The modern way of saying it is they are drifters who are just what their environment makes them. If they had some great beacon light of a high ideal always in sight, they wouldn't be turned so easily.

———

Goals? The Church has but one goal, despite the fact that the auxiliaries sometimes seem to be competing with each other for activity. The great goal of the Church is to make each individual worthy to attain life eternal.

GOD

Ask any Christian in the world if he thinks the Lord rules and reigns supreme in heaven, and he will tell you, "Yes."

Is it right for the Lord to reign? "Certainly it is."

Ask him if he would delight to live in a place where one character rules and reigns supreme, and he will answer, "Yes, if I could go to heaven."

Why? "Why, the Lord reigns there."

Just ask the Christian if he knows the Lord, and he will tell you, "No."

Did you ever see him? "No."

Can you tell me anything of his character? "No, only he is something without body, parts, and passions."

One of the apostles says that "God is love, and they who dwell in God dwell in love."

Ask the Christian world if they know anything about God and they will tell you that they do not. Ask if he has eyes, and they will say, "No,—yes he is all eyes."

Has he a head? "Yes, he is all head."

Has he ears? "Yes, he is all ears, he is all mouth, he is all body, and all limbs," and still without body, parts, or passions.

Why what do they make of him. A monster, if he is anything, that is what they make of him.

Would you like to go to heaven? "O yes," says the Christian, "the Lord reigns there."

How do you know you would like the place and the order when you get there? Do you think you will have your farm and your substance by yourself, and live in the gratification of your selfish propensities as you now do? "O, no, we expect to be made pure and holy."

Where will you begin to be pure and holy? If you do not begin here, I do not know where you will begin. "O," says the Christian, "if we are going to heaven, where God and angels dwell, and live where one-man power prevails, we should be satisfied, I expect."

We Latter-day Saints say so, too. We like to see that power manifested by those whom God calls to lead the people in righteousness, purity, and holiness.

—President Brigham Young

———

We children, we men and women, who for the time being have to learn like little boys and girls, by crude and primitive methods—we are told that the time will come when, as the reward of obedience, of continued faithfulness, our bodies shall be filled with light, our eyes be single to the glory of God. But we approach that condition gradually. We are learning how to do things little by little. We do them now in inferior ways; but our Heavenly Father has learned how to do them in a masterful way. Then why should we seek to drag him down, and deny his power to do things that we are not able to do? Where is the logic of it?

—Elder Orson F. Whitney

———

In a revelation concerning a tried people, the Lord said to the Prophet Joseph Smith on December 16, 1833:

"Yet I will own them, and they shall be mine in that day when I shall come to make up my jewels." (D&C 101:3.)

Commenting upon the passage, Elder James E. Talmage of the Council of the Twelve said in general conference, October 1921:

"The Lord . . . loves jewels, but they must be genuine. No colored glass for rubies, no mere paste for diamonds, they must be the real thing; and when he comes to make up his jewels, I would rather be found a little tiny one-hundredth of a caret diamond than a glass imitation the size of the Culinam, the biggest diamond ever found. The Lord help us to be what we seem to be, before him, before our brethren, and in our own consciences, I humbly pray. . . ."

HABIT

Habit is a powerful factor in the makeup of character; as our habits are, so are we judged. If we are kind and thoughtful by nature, our habits will prove the fact. The habit of doing good or evil will distinguish the individual according to the forces he puts into it, and if that habit can find circumstances to develop it, it may have a wide influence.

———————

"A prisoner has escaped the state penitentiary by going over the wall," the newscaster said. And we knew that sometime, perhaps on the next newscast, it would be reported that the prisoner had been recaptured. There is no more sure thing in the world.

And we know, too, that we are prisoners of ourselves. We never get away from ourselves, or the walls we build for ourselves, for long. We can only tear down the bad walls within ourselves and, often using the same material, construct the good walls of habit just where they should be.

———————

HAPPINESS

What Goldsmith wrote as a criticism on the French people may be safely considered one of the laws of happiness:

"They please, are pleased, they give to get esteem;
Till, seeming blest, they grow to what they seem."

Real happiness comes from doing for others
and in blessing others. Sacrificing, in the end is not
a sacrifice, but the winning of a prize—salvation.

—President Charles W. Nibley

———

"First I got tired, then I got retired, and then I
got untired," said a grand old high priest, great in
his humility, during priesthood class one Sabbath
morning. "I got tired because I figured out that
happiness and satisfaction have as their base the
number of good things that a person responds to."

———

HOLY GHOST

True faith in God, repentance true;
Sins remitted by immersion;
The humble soul is born anew
And the Spirit takes possession.
By laying on of holy hands
Of God's own servants here on earth,
Those who've obeyed the Lord's commands
Will realize the Spirit's birth.

—From "The Gospel Pioneer"
by Elder William Jefferies

———

The sun shines upon the evil and the good; but the Holy Ghost descends only upon the righteous and upon those that are forgiven of their sins. The rain descends upon the evil and upon the good; but the rights of the priesthood are conferred, and the doctrine of the priesthood distills as the dews of heaven upon the souls of those only that receive it in God's own appointed way. The favor of heaven, the acknowledgement of the Almighty of his children upon the earth as his sons and his daughters can only be secured through obedience to the laws which he has revealed.

—President Joseph F. Smith

———

HUMILITY

The Ba'al Shem Tov, whose birth was in 1700, told of a high government official who, although extremely wealthy and prominent, got no joy out of life. Any untoward incident or frustration caused him great inner torment, and often brought him to the point of utter exhaustion. He worried about wasting away his days. He brooded over some humiliation which he had suffered long ago. At times the fear of death overwhelmed him. He sought out doctors, but their medicines did not help. He counseled with wise men whose advice gave him no comfort.

Once a poor beggar visited him and saw that he was extremely sad. When the beggar asked him why he was so despondent, the official told him some of the fears which oppressed him, and for which he could find no cure.

The old man then said to him: "I have a medicine for you. Know that the source of all the sadness which afflicts you is the arrogance which is in your heart. In your pride you think that the whole world belongs to you, that all the good of the world should go to you, and that you deserve immortality. But surely you will die as everyone else. You will not be cured from your illness until you are happy with your lot. Then, and only then, will you no longer know any sadness."

The official took the advice of the old man seriously. From that time on he would not sit in his carriage, since he knew very well that this was a source of pride for him. Instead he walked after the carriage on foot, muttering to himself, "I am humble. I am walking by foot, and the carriage is in front of me."

A long time afterward, the beggar met him on the road and saw him doing this. He said to him: "My lord, this is not the way to achieve humility. Sit rather in the carriage in a way which will exemplify humility. Then the humility will be not merely on your lips, and in your thoughts, but also etched on your heart. This humility is the most difficult to achieve."

———

One of these days I must go shopping. I am completely out of self-respect. I want to exchange the self-righteousness I picked up the other day for some humility which they say is less expensive and wears better.

I want to look at some tolerance which is being used for wraps this season. Someone showed me some pretty samples of peace. We are a little low on that and one can never have too much of it.

And, by the way, I must try to match some patience that my neighbor wears. It is very becoming to her and I think it might look well on me.

Also, I must not forget to have my sense of humor mended.

And I must look for some inexpensive everyday goodness. It is surprising how quickly one's stock of goodness is depleted.

Yes, I must go shopping!

—Anonymous

———

KNOWLEDGE

On the view of continuing education lasting as long as life, Elder Richard L. Evans of the Council of the Twelve related this to a devotional assembly at Brigham Young University in 1963:

" 'How much did you learn?' the father asked of his son returning home from his first day attending kindergarten.

" 'Not enough,' the youngster replied. 'I've got to go back tomorrow.' "

———

Many ideas grow better when transplanted into another mind than in the one where they sprang up. That which was a weed in one intelligence becomes a flower in the other, and a flower again dwindles down to a mere weed by the same change. Healthy growth may become poisonous by falling upon the wrong mental soil, and what seemed a night-shade in one mind unfolds as a morning-glory in another.

———

LEADERSHIP

" 'No pack camel will continue to go forward unless something is leading him.' " Brother Ben stood tall at the pulpit and smiled. "Or so I read in an old magazine the other night. Even today as a caravan moves in the great deserts of the Middle East, someone in the party has the important task of constantly moving between the pack animals, seeing that each camel's rope is securely tied to the camel before him. Then out front, hand securely on the lead-rope, is the man who leads the camel caravan.

"Now, surely we are more than camels. We are the people of the Lord, called to accomplish his purposes upon the earth. In the scriptures we are often called sheep and are led by the Son, the Good Shepherd.

"But: 'No pack camel will continue to go forward unless something is leading him.' That bit of information continues to intrigue me. How often we, ourselves, can go astray when we forget the leadership before us for a moment. And so, it seems to me, that we are all tied together with the proper ropes, the programs of the Church. Out front, striding in the forward motion, hand fully on the programs, is the President of the Church. the Prophet of God in this generation. Wherever he leads, we follow, even as we are tied in by the proper ropes—the programs of the Church."

———

The leader must be luminous; he must see ahead. It is expected that he will see farther and better than any or all of those whose activities he is expected to direct. The very suspicion that a leader is behind the times is to be dreaded. A great general once said, "If I am to direct this army, I must know the way better than any soldier."

Preparation for leadership must be progressive. The leader must be a student as well as an executive. He must study books as well as men, intellectual preparation, demonstrating by a kind of knowledge wider and deeper than the demands of routine work. There must be a reserve with which to meet the unexpected. Intellectual preparation for mutual improvement leadership demands a specialist in each special line of leadership. Each leader may know a little of everything, but he must know everything of something, and that particular something is that in which he is called to lead.

The wise leader must be a specialist on the manual, his knowledge of it must be more than the combined knowledge of the class. And so with other departments. Preparation for intellectual leadership demands obedience to the command: "Seek ye out of the best books words of wisdom."

Another source of intellectual preparation for leadership is the council meeting. Exchange of ideas always increases intellectual illumination. Preparation for leadership demands that the labor shall be decisive; and decision, to be respected, must be based upon information.

The exercise of faith strengthens the spiritual man, and it does more. It brings about a re-enforcement of the soul from without. An inspired man is all of himself plus the inspiration of God. The scripture which says, "Seek ye learning by study and also by faith," is an invitation to draw upon the fountain of divine intelligence. Spiritual preparation for leadership requires that a man should be possessed of the assurance that "the Lord giveth no commandment to the children of men save he shall prepare a way for them that they may accomplish the thing which he commandeth them." And that preparation, too, must be progressive.

Keeping up official as well as private correspondence with the Lord is a source of development of spiritual leadership, and our correspondence is wireless. We call it prayer. It is not only a privilege but a duty. To call upon the Lord, in preparation for leadership, doing the very best we can, like one who plants in season with faith, cultivates with care, and leaves to the Lord the increase, is progressive preparation for leadership. Believing as did the boy prophet: "If any man lack wisdom, let him ask of God," is good preparation for leadership. Recognizing also one's inability to do his best alone, as did Joseph in Egypt, when he said to Pharaoh, "It is not in me," and then exerting the faith within, as did Joseph—"God shall give Pharaoh an answer of peace."

The attitude expressed in the following make good moral preparation: "I will be what I would have my followers become." "I will be more exacting of myself than I will be of my followers." A great leader in his life adopted this motto: "No man shall be more exacting of me than I am of myself." That was my beloved teacher, Brother Karl G. Maeser.

"It shall be my highest aim to be worthy of the approval of those I follow, and the confidence of those who follow me." That is expressive of an inward preparation for leadership.

—Elder George H. Brimhall
(June Conference 1914)

LIFE

The great prizes of life do not fall to the most brilliant, to the cleverest, to the shrewdest, to the most long-headed, or to the best educated, but to the most level-headed men, to the men of soundest judgment. When a man is wanted for responsible position, his shrewdness is not considered so important as his sound judgment. Reliability is what is wanted. Can a man stand without being tripped; and if he is thrown, can he land on his feet? Can he be depended upon, relied upon under all circumstances to do the right thing, the sensible thing? Has the man a level head? Has he "good horse sense"? Is he liable to fly off on a tangent or "go off half-cocked"? Is he "faddy"? Has he "wheels in his head"? Does he lose his temper easily, or can he control himself? If he can keep a level head under all circumstances, if he cannot be thrown off his balance, and is honest, he is the man wanted.

———

Some complain that life is difficult and that if there was a second chance they'd do better. But, with tongue in cheek, many of the television programs are played and replayed and replayed. Those programs play for the first time during a cold winter night, when weather and other conditions may be so difficult that a convenient excuse could be had for practically anything. The reruns are made usually during the summer, when the weather presents ideal conditions. But, watching the original runs and the reruns, the things become familiar and the end results—no matter how many times those programs breathlessly unfold, the end is always the same as at first.

And we wonder if, given a second chance, our actions in mortality would be exactly the same as the first time.

"The two greatest days of your life," said a speaker, "are the day you were born and the day you found out why you were born."

It is not the briefness of our lives; it is our lost opportunities.

Education is the proper employment, not only of our early years, but of our whole life.

Our past life is not past; it lives in at least two ways: in the character we have formed and in the influence we have exerted. All life is a springtime of sowing; in due season we shall reap. Heaven lies hidden in our daily deeds, even as the oak with all its centuries of growth and all its summer glory sleeps in the acorn cup.

LOVE

Is love blind? Our cynical friends tell us it is. But I do not agree. Love is the only thing that sees. Where would you be today if someone who loved you did not see things in you that nobody else saw?

Who but your mother thought you were the finest baby ever born; And why did she have faith in you when no one else did? Because love saw.

Then the best girl in the world said she'd marry you—even though her friends asked one another: "What did she see in him?" Love saw.

When things were so black you even lost faith in yourself, a great-hearted man or woman became your friend and pulled you through. Why? Because love saw.

There is something fine and big in every one of us, but only those who love can see it. Who can say love is blind?

—Anonymous

———————

The bishop and his auxiliary heads were admiring recently purchased equipment in their ward library: the books, files of pictures, flannelboards, projectors, duplicating devices, and the rest.

Then the bishop mused aloud, "Brothers and sisters, these are wonderful, all of them; I am glad that they are here, but until someone can produce a machine that can create and apply love, your teachers in the classes can never be replaced."

———————

What is Love?

It's silence when your words would hurt,
It's patience when your neighbor's curt,
It's defense when the scandal flows,
It's thoughtfulness for another's woes,
It's promptness when stern duty calls,
It's courage when misfortune falls.

—Anonymous

———————

Could we look into the hearts concealed from us, we should often pity where we hate, love where we think we can never forgive, and admire where we curl the lip with scorn and indignation.

MAN

God made a computer once, constructing it with infinite care and precision exceeding that of all the scientists combined. Using clay for the main structure, he installed within it a system for the continuous intake of information of all kinds and descriptions, by sight, hearing, and feeling; a circulatory system to preserve its strength and vigor in perpetuity; and a nervous system to keep all parts in constant communication and coordination. Lying there on the ground in Eden, it far surpassed the finest modern computer and was equally dead. It was equipped to memorize and calculate and work with the most complex equation, but there was something lacking.

Then God drew near and "breathed into his nostrils the breath of life; and man became a living soul." (Gen. 2:7.)

That is why man has powers no modern computer possesses or ever will possess. God gave

man life and with it the power to think and reason
and decide and love. With such power given to you
and to me, mastery of self becomes a necessity if
we are to have the abundant life.

—Elder Thomas S. Monson

————

A sage once said: "Man's age-old problem is
that he desires to please himself rather than God."

————

Not numerous years nor lengthened life
Nor pretty children nor a wife;
Nor pins and chains and fancy rings;
Nor any such-like trumpery things,
Nor pipes, cigars, nor bottled wine;
Nor liberty with kings to dine;
Nor coat nor boot, nor yet a hat,
A dandy vest or trim cravat;
Nor master, reverend sir, nor squire,
With titles that the memory tire;
Nor ancestry tracked back to Will
Who went from Normandy to kill;
Nor judge's robe nor mayor's mace,
Nor crown that decks the royal race;
These, all united, never can
Enlarge the soul to make the man.

A truthful soul, a loving mind
Full of affection for its kind;
A helper of the human race,
A soul of beauty and of grace;
A spirit firm, erect and free,
That never basely bends the knee;
That will not bear a feather's weight
Of slavery's chain for small or great;
That firmly speaks of God within,
And never makes a league with sin;
That snaps the fetters despots make
That loves the truth for its own sake;
That worships God and only God,
That trembles at no tyrant's nod—
And thus can smile in curse and ban—
That is the soul that makes the man.

—Anonymous

———

Woman was created from the rib of man,
She was not made from his head—to top him;
Nor out of his feet, to be trampled upon;
But out of his side, to be equal to him;
Under his arm, to be protected;
And near his heart, to be loved.

—Anonymous

———

MISSIONARIES

The way in which the gospel message is carried into an area is sometimes marvelous. Here is a now little-known incident. Writing from the Scandinavian Mission to the *Deseret News,* in a letter dated March 27, 1910, Elder Franklin J. D. Jensen said from Egersund, Norway:

"Some months ago a vessel en route from mission headquarters in Copenhagen to Trondhjem, Norway, was stranded near Hangesund, Norway. It carried several packages of tracts for the Latter-day Saints' office at Bergen. By some means or other some of these tracts were kept afloat after the shipwreck and one package was found at Skudenaess on the island of Carman, by a fisherman. Several days after this another package was found by another fisherman while fishing off the coast about a hundred English miles south, near Eher Island. The tracts were, of course, well soaked, but were taken to the fisherman's hut and dried by the old fashioned fireplace.

"On investigation the people discovered that the tracts contained interesting information and explanations of different verses of the Bible, and they were so deeply interested that they distributed them and each family in that vicinity got some tracts."

A short time afterwards Elder Jensen came to that area and began distributing his leaflets. What was his surprise when he learned that the wind and the waves had already carried the message to these people. He heard the story of the shipwreck and was shown the tracts, "Leaves of Truth," by Elder, later President, Charles W. Penrose. Some of the fishermen and their families desired to hear more from the missionary then among them.

———

There are many millions of people in the world who count themselves Christian and who undoubtedly have deep and sincere faith in the spiritual realm of our Lord. I could wish that we might look upon all such good men and women as of Zion and that they might be considered as having come out of the world. This would please me because it seems so broadminded, so tolerant, and so neighborly.

My theology teaches me, however, that I cannot be quite so liberal and I am constrained by the plain revelation of our Father to say to my Christian brother, however indelicate it may seem to utter it:

"I believe you to be good; I acknowledge your sincerity; I am grateful for the faith you have; I esteem your good works; but it is my duty to tell you that there is a higher order of things than you have yet embraced, that more light and knowledge have been given than you have received. When you have accepted this higher order which embraces the fullness of the gospel of our Lord, and then only, is it possible for you to come into Zion and truly be of the fold of Christ."

—President Stephen L Richards

———

Every man is a missionary now and forever, for good or for evil—whether he intends or designs it or not. He may be a blot, radiating in dark influence outward to the very circumference of society; or he may be a blessing, spreading benediction over the length and breadth of the world; but a blank he cannot be. There are no moral blanks; there are no neutral persons. We are either the darkness that sows and corrupts, or the light that splendidly illuminates, and the salt that silently operates; but being dead or alive, every man speaks.

———

There is a truism ever active: "Those who hear the gospel must obey it, or they cannot be saved by it."

———

While pursuing my missionary labors I went to a house and knocked. A fine looking, dignified lady answered and I told her the purpose of my visit. I explained that I was a missionary of The Church of Jesus Christ of Latter-day Saints and I asked if I might have the privilege of explaining to her some of the principles of the gospel which the Church taught. To my surprise, she immediately became angry and indignantly said to me, "I resent your bringing the gospel to me. I'm as good a Christian as ever you dare be. I've always been a member of a Christian church and supported the Christian cause. Take your gospel to the heathen!"

I said to her: "Madam, will you permit me to ask a few questions?"

She said: "What are they?"

"In your study of the gospel, have you ever discovered the way which work may be done for your kindred dead?"

"No;" she did not know it was necessary.

"Have you ever been told of a power that can bind you and your husband together beyond this life when 'death doth you part,' and also assure you of the companionship of your children in the family relationship in the life to come?"

No; she had never heard of such a power, although she hoped for a reunion hereafter.

"Have the various kingdoms or gradations that exist in heaven ever been explained to you?"

"No, never."

"What is the difference between salvation and exaltation? What has God stated the purpose of man's life to be? What is the Christian doctrine of eternal progression?"

She did not know. Her resentment subsided.

She said, "Young man, I beg your pardon. I see there is much about the gospel I do not know. Won't you please come in and explain?"

—A report of a returned missionary
recalled by
President Stephen L Richards

MONEY

An ambitious young man had enjoyed himself as the dinner guest of the wealthiest family in town. Finishing his dessert, he turned to his host, asking: "Tell me, sir, how did you get your wealth?"

"It's a long story that I'll be pleased to share with you. But first let me blow out the candle; there's no sense in wasting the wax!"

A shrewd old gentleman once said to his daughter:

"Be sure, my dear, you never marry a poor man."

"Father, you speak in parables very well," she replied. "You have often said that the poorest man in the world is one that has money and nothing else."

There are many worse and longer sermons than the following upon the text, "It is more blessed to give than to receive":

"I've known many a church to die because it didn't give enough, but I have never known a church to die because it gave too much. Churches don't die that way. Brethren, have any of you known a church to die because it gave too much? If you do, just let me know, and I will make a pilgrimage to that church, and I'll stand there and

lift up my hands to heaven and say, 'Blessed are
the dead that die in the Lord.' "

————

MUSIC

Music gives us courage on life's uneven highway.

Music cheers the faint and weary.

Music lulls the babe into dreamland.

Music makes the heart tender.

Music smoothes the passage to the grave.

Music refines the home and draws the family
together in tender sentiments of reverence and
aspiration.

Music awakens heroic virtues and arouses in the
sluggish breast, enthusiasm.

Music gives a distinctive force in social ranks.

Music stirs the soul and unfolds the mental
vision to the highest ideals of character.

Music! Without its divine power, human life
would fade away and men and women become
automatons, heartless and cold.

—John Phillips Meakin

[There are many stories of the great Mormon
Pioneer hymn, "Come, Come Ye Saints" being
sung in many places and in many climes. Here is
one story:]

In the year 1921, before the amplification of
sound and the flinging of it in a twinkling over
continent and sea and into outer space, a family
lived a half-mile from the grandstand at Liberty
Park in Salt Lake City.

It was announced that the Salt Lake Tabernacle
Choir would sing there at the park on Pioneer Day
and the young mother desired with all her heart to
be there to hear them. But the baby took sick with
dreaded "summer complaint," and for several days
and nights required tender nursing. All Pioneer
Day the mother stayed close to her baby. Then at
dusk the baby seemed better and the mother went
to the front porch for a breath of air.

She glanced in the direction of the park and
realized that this had been the day of the

Tabernacle Choir concert. It was about the time for the singing of the final number. She thought again of her baby as a cooling breeze came up. And on that breeze came the words in the voice of the Choir: "All is well, all is well."

She hesitated. There was no breeze and no words now. But in another moment the Choir would be singing that phrase again. And at that moment the gentle breeze was there again with the assurance from the Tabernacle Choir: "All is well, all is well."

She bowed her head in thanksgiving. Then she returned inside the house to find that all was truly well with her baby.

———

NEW YEARS

Ring out the old, ring in the new,
    Ring, happy bells, across the snow;
The year is going, let him go;
    Ring out the false, ring in the true.

—Alfred, Lord Tennyson

———

There is a saying of Benjamin Franklin:

> "Be at War with your Vices,
> at Peace with your Neighbors,
> and let every New-Year
> find you a better man."

The tide of life on which we move, like gently rolling hills, seems to rise and fall, and as we reach the summit of each New Year we stop to review the past, and to look into the future, before plunging forward into the mystic valley of life's activities.

—Elder John G. McQuarrie

OBEDIENCE

Have you ever thought of the fact that there is a power, an actual force, a definite form of energy, in obedience? That energy is just as real as the force that is giving light to these lamps serving in the hours of darkness to illuminate this great [Tabernacle] for us. I think we shall yet come to recognize the force, the power, the energy, that lies in obedience. We have many demonstrations of it.

I have been impressed with the fact that the scientific spirit, as man calls it, is manifest in the organization of the Church and its operation. It is only through obedience to what we call the forces of nature, the laws of energy, that we are able to make them serve our purposes. We would have none of these lights unless we obeyed strictly, with full purpose of heart, the laws of electricity.

Yesterday morning, between nine and ten o'clock, we heard in this city the very voice of the Premier of Great Britain who had just landed at the port of New York. [This was October 1929—and we wonder at what the speaker's reaction would be if he had witnessed what we have forty years later—not only the sound but the sight of space exploration.] How was that miracle made possible? Through strict obedience to the laws by which the energy was employed and then applied through the radio, and in none other way would the marvel have been wrought. We have to obey the laws of light, the laws of mechanical construction, and the laws of chemistry if we would operate the camera successfully and get good pictures. That time-piece yonder would be worth nothing had not the laws of mechanics been very strictly obeyed in its construction. It is only through obedience to law that we enjoy blessings.

—Elder James E. Talmage

OFFERINGS

A man purchased a field and hid his treasure there. He went silently, lest, if he made a great bluster, some other individual might go and steal the march on him and purchase the field of treasure, then the bargain would have been complete; but no, he was wide awake, and sold all that he had and purchased that field, for he was determined to have that treasure. It took all he had to purchase it, but the treasure concealed there was far beyond the cost of purchase value, and in purchasing it he knew that it would increase in time and throughout all eternity, for that treasure was the kingdom of God, and salvation to that man's soul. [That is a re-telling of Matthew 13:44.]

A question comes up in the minds of some: I have frequently heard persons say, "What becomes of our tithing? And what is the propriety from this quarter and calls from that; and what are we doing when we are buying that field in which the treasure lies concealed?"

Did we ever think, when responding to the calls on the right and on the left, that we were purchasing that field, and that having gone to the extent of our power and ability in that transaction, that there is our deed and title to the kingdom of God, signed, sealed and delivered? ... The kingdom is ours. We have purchased it, and by it our salvation is secured, by faithfulness in the kingdom.

—Elder Orson Hyde

In summing up a phase of a discussion on fasting and fast offerings, a wise old patriarch said: "These are the meals that belong to the Lord."

OPINION

"What will other people think?" is the most cowardly phrase in use by society.

Only weak men stand in fear of the censure of the neighborhood.

Whatever is great in life brings down some censure at first upon the head of the doer.

Why not dress your life before your own mirror?

Look for your reflections in your own mind. There is a secret judge of all your acts within you. Conscience is, in part, your private opinion of yourself.

Why borrow a thing when you possess it yourself? What does it matter what others think of your actions? What do *you* think of them? Are they right?

Some men crouch, crawl, and skulk all their lives. They are cowed by a whisper; their purpose is shaken by a look. They run like sheep before somebody's opinion, though they would return blow for blow if they were attacked on the highway.

They are greased and curled wax figures. Whenever they move you know that Public Opinion has pulled a wire somewhere. When they speak you know what they will say. They are not men enough to offend.

The ogre, Public Opinion, slays more originality and individuality than all the barbarous superstitious codes put together. It is the modern Moloch before which we all meekly bend.

That shameful hypocrisy which permeates society everywhere is born of the fear of other people's opinions. Sincerity and plain speaking are at a premium everywhere. We lie from morning until night, and pretend to things we knowingly abhor.

Turn once upon that lazy braggart, Public Opinion, and see it scamper away.

It is our idol that is always with us, the modern social Juggernaut.

—Benjamin De Casseres

————

OPPORTUNITIES

Satan tried it in the great councils of heaven. He proposed that the plan for mortality be changed there and then so that all men would trade opportunity for security.

————

The story is told of an Indian farmer named Ali Hafid who could neither read nor write, but who was fortunate enough to have his own farm, his own bullock, a fine wife, and a good family.

In India the fakirs are traveling monks who beg among the people, write letters for them, and tell them the latest news. One day a fakir came to Ali Hafid and told him of a marvelous discovery recently made of a stone called a "diamond" which was most valuable as a jewel because it shone as though the sun were captured inside it shooting forth beams of colored light.

The story so caught the imagination of Ali Hafid that he sold his farm and house and left his wife and family to search for diamonds. He traveled far and wide searching, but never found the precious stones. Finally, broken in body and spirit, having exhausted his funds in his fruitless search, he cast himself into the sea, and drowned.

About that time the fakir came through the village again and stopped at the farm formerly owned by Ali Hafid and there on the mantelplace he saw a lovely diamond.

"I see Ali found his diamond," he said, pointing to the stone.

"Oh, Ali sold me his farm," said the new owner, "and that stone is just a pretty rock I found down in the streambed as I watered my sheep."

"Show me the place," said the fakir, and the man led him to the stream.

There in the gravel bottom of the streambed they found one diamond after another. A further search showed the whole farm contained dia-

monds, even in the dirt floor in the cellar of the
house. The story claims that thus the rich Gol-
conda diamond field was discovered. There be-
neath his very feet was the fortune for which Ali
Hafid gave his life in a fruitless search.

———

Perhaps the reason for many lost opportunities
may be explained by this little couplet of verse:

> "We look too high
> For things close by."

———

ORDER

Comfort is the daughter of order, and is
descended in a direct line from wisdom; she is
closely allied to carefulness, thrift, honesty, and
she has been educated by good sense, benevolence,
observation and experience; and she is the mother
of cleanliness, economy, provident forethought,
virtue, propriety, and domestic happiness.

Muddle is descended from the ancient but
dishonorable family of chaos; she is the child of
indifference, and want of principle, educated
alternately by dawdling hurry, stupidity, obsti-

nacy, meanness, and extravagance, secretely united at an early age to self-conceit, and parent of procrastination, falsehood, dirt, waste, disorder, destruction, and desolation.

PARENTS

J. Edgar Hoover, head of the Federal Bureau of Investigation, explained that juvenile delinquency seldom if ever comes from homes in which:

1.   Parents try to understand their children and find time to cultivate their friendship and love.

2.   Parents of integrity face facts and live by the truth.

3.   Parents live within their means and give their children examples in thrift, security, and stability.

4.   Parents are industrious and teach their children that most of life's good things come only from hard work.

5.   Parents have worthwhile goals in life and

seek to have their children join them in their attainment.

6.   Parents have common sense, and a capacity for friendship and a sense of humor.

7.   Parents live in harmony with each other and do not quarrel in the presence of their children.

8.   Parents have ideals and a compelling urge to serve rather than to be served.

9.   Parents are unswervingly loyal to their own children, but can express righteous indignation and chastise them when necessary. (That old proverb "Spare the rod and spoil the child" is as vital today as it ever was.)

10.   Parents' decisions are controlled, not by what their children desire, but what they need.

PATHWAYS

There is a path which can be trod
That leads us back to Father God;
The Holy Ghost directs the way,
Each one must work as well as pray.

The path which leads to that great goal
Is one that's laid for every soul;
'Twas Christ who made and set the plan
'Twas it he preached and taught to man.

No boast, no pomp, can reach its end,
No pride, no wealth can e'er ascend;
But noble thoughts and humble deeds,
A truthful, prayerful heart it needs.

Now, can we walk there in a day?
Old Patience calmly answers "nay."
And then he wisely tells us, too,
To work and wait till life is through.

—D. W. Parratt

One day at a time! That's all it can be.
   No faster than that is the hardest fate,
And days have their limits, however we
   Begin them too early and stretch them late.

One day at a time! Every heart that aches
   Knows only too well how long that can seem;
But it's never today which the spirit breaks,
   It's the darkened future, without a gleam.

One day at a time! A burden too late
   To be borne for two, can be born for one;
Who knows what will enter tomorrow's gate?
   While yet we are speaking, all may be done.

One day at a time! What joy is at height—
    Such joy as the heart can never forget—
And pulses are throbbing with wild delight,
    How hard to remember that suns must set!

One day at a time! But a single day,
    Whatever its load, whatever its length;
And there's a bit of precious scripture to say
    That according to each shall be our strength.

One day at a time! 'Tis the whole of life!
    All sorrow, all joy, are measured therein.
The bound of our purpose, our noblest strife,
    The one only countersign, sure to win!

—Helen Hunt Jackson

———

"Your way is dark," the Angel said,
    "Because you downward gaze:
Look up; the sun is overhead.
    Look up and learn to praise."
I looked: I learned. Who looks above
Will find in Heaven both Light and Love.

"Why upward gaze?" the Angel said:
    "Have you not learned to know
The light of God shines overhead
    That men may work below?"
I learned. Who only looks above
May miss below the work of love.

And then I learned the lessons twain:
    The heart whose treasure is above
Will gladly turn to earth again
    Because the Heaven is Love.
Yes, Love that framed the starry height
Came down to Earth and gave it Light.

          —The Bishop of Ripon

PEACE

To be glad of life because it gives you the chance to love and to work and to play and to look to the stars. To be satisfied with your possessions but not contented with yourself until you have made the most of them. To despise nothing in the world except falsehood and meanness, and to fear nothing but cowardice. To be governed by your admirations rather than your disgusts; to covet nothing that is your neighbor's except his kindness of heart and gentleness of manner. To think seldom of your enemies, often of your friends, and every day of Christ; and to spend as much time as you can with body and with spirit, in God's out-of-doors. These are little guideposts on the footpaths to peace.

          —Henry Van Dyke

In most quarrels there is fault on both sides. As the pioneers used to say: "Both flint and steel are necessary to the production of a spark. Either of them may hammer on wood forever, and no fire will follow."

PRAYER

In all your troubles, go to the Lord for help; in all your joys, go to the Lord in praise and thanksgiving.

—Elder George H. Brimhall

I asked God for strength that I might achieve,
   I was made weak that I might learn humbly
      to obey.
I asked for wealth that I might do greater
   things.
   I was given infirmity that I might do better
      things.
I asked for riches that I might be happy,
   I was given poverty that I might be wise.
I asked for power that I might have the praise
   of men,
   I was given weakness that I might feel the
      need of God.

I asked for all things that I might enjoy life,
   I was given life that I might enjoy all things.
I got nothing that I asked for,
   But everything I had hoped for.
Almost despite myself, my unspoken prayers
   were answered.
   I am among all men most richly blessed!

—Said to have been found on the body of
         an Unknown Confederate Soldier

———

A soul without prayer is like a solitary sheep without its shepherd. The tempter sees it, and lures it away into his snares.

———

A while ago a robber, in preparation for his crime, took the precaution to cut the telephone wires that were serving the building of his intended victims, knowing full well that they then could not call for and receive aid.

But how many of us have neighbors, or even ourselves, who voluntarily sever the lines of communication with our Heavenly Father by neglecting to say our prayers? Surely that self-sin is as great as the preparatory act of the robber who cuts the telephone lines of his intended victims.

———

PRIESTHOOD

[President George A. Smith, Counselor to President Brigham Young, recalled the testimony of Oliver Cowdery, at the time that Brother Cowdery rejoined the Church. Oliver said:]

"When the Saints follow the main channel of the stream, they find themselves in deep water and always right, pursuing their journey with safety; but when they turn aside into sloughs and bayous, they are left to flounder in the mud and are lost, for the Angel of God said unto Joseph in my hearing that this Priesthood shall remain on the earth until the end."

———

Our Heavenly Father is desirous to promote the happiness and welfare of the whole human family; and if we, any of us, hold any priesthood, it is simply for that same purpose, and not for our personal aggrandizement, or for our honor, or pomp, or position; but we hold it in the interest of God and for the salvation of the people, that through it we may promote their happiness, blessing, and prosperity, temporal and spiritual, both here and in the world to come. That is why the priesthood is conferred upon us, and if we do not use in in this way, then there is a malfeasance in office; then we violate our obligations before God, and render ourselves unworthy of that high calling that the Lord has conferred upon us. The priesthood always was given for the blessing of the human family. People talk about it as though it was for the special benefit of individuals.

—President John Taylor

PROCRASTINATION

Though Nathan faced a task and knew
    He should begin it.
He could not start to put it through
    For "just a minute."
And, though the case demanded speed,
He could not move just then; but he'd
Be ready for it, yes, indeed!
    In "just a minute."

His purposes were not of rhyme
    By "just a minute."
The whole world seemed ahead of time
    By "just a minute."
He could not learn to overhaul
His many duties large and small,
But had to beg them, one and all,
    To "wait a minute."

In manhood he was still delayed
    By "just a minute."
He might have won, had Fortune stayed
    For "just a minute."
But at the end of life he railed
At cruel Fate, and wept and wailed
Because he knew that he had failed
    By "just a minute."

—Nixon Waterman

———

The day is gone, and what have I done?
What have I gained, or what have I won?
    The sun sinks down in a golden sea;
Long shadows creep over the meadow and hill;
The world of labor grows silent and still;
    But what has the past day brought to me?

What have I done for my soul today?
What have I done that will me repay?
    What have I added unto myself?
How much of truth has with me grown?
How much that I may call my own—
    Of real worth, and not of pelf?

What have I done, O Lord, for Thee?
How have I helped to set men free
    From evil thoughts and lives of sin?

The day is gone—and may I say:
"One struggling soul I've helped today
   Eternal life and light to win"?

—Anonymous

RELIGION

There is nothing selfish in religion; the more
you give away, the more you have. If you can keep
all your religion to yourself, you may be sure that
you have a religion that is not worth having.

A. A. Ellis, writing in an old *Millennial Star,*
said:

"Let us consider the sectarian views as photo-
graphic pictures, and then we need not accuse
anyone of having defective sight; but we can say
that such photographs are taken on a cloudy and
misty day, when objects are indistinct so that the
retoucher must needs make the picture present-
able, no matter how deceptive or untrue it may be.
He does not see the original, but in order to please
the people and insure his employment he makes
the pictures look good at a distance.

"After the retouching we compare the photographs with the original building and find as follows: A window light is obliterated; inspiration and revelation are no more considered necessary; but man's wisdom supplants the necessary influence and inspiration of the Holy Ghost. In consequence we have doubt and uncertainty. . . ."

Then he asked:

"Can we make a building as good as the original from our defective or indistinct photographs as a pattern, or must we seek the divine guidance of the heavenly Architect? What plans have we to build from? What material shall we place in the foundation? Have we authority to build?

He answers his questions:

"We cannot build according to our indistinct photographs and make a complete building as constructed by God through his Son Jesus Christ upon the rock of revelation. Manmade additions and omissions will not frame a perfect structure. To perfect the structure, we must have the essential parts and also authority from the heavens. God's house is a house of order, and must be built according to the divine pattern.

———

REPENTANCE

Repentance is an evidence
Of living, saving faith in God.
The sinner manifesting sense
In turning from the path he trod—
Not a sentimental sorrow,
Felt today and gone tomorrow;
But—by God's help I will do right,
And shun all wrong with all my might.

—From "The Gospel Pioneer"
by Elder William Jeffries

———

RESTORATION

O how the world ought to rejoice that in this day that which so long has been lost has been restored, the fullness of the gospel, the power and authority of the Holy Priesthood, the doctrines of the Church, and not only that but the organization of the Church as well in its perfection and in its power.

When I think of the efforts of men to rebuild the church—and I do not want to belittle their efforts—I do not blame them. I believe that Joseph Smith and his associates could not have done any better than Martin Luther, nor than John Wesley or others, except for the fact that the Lord revealed himself to him. I do not belittle the efforts of these men who did the best they could with the light and knowledge which they had, but their knowledge was limited.

Their effort to rebuild and establish the Church of Christ reminds me of the experience I had with my first watch. I wanted to see what it was made of, so I took it to pieces, and I had so many wheels that when I tried to put it together again I could not get all those wheels within that case. I put in as many as I could and it looked like a watch all right; but it did not serve the purpose for which a watch is made, to keep the time. Every wheel was important and necessary.

And so men have tried to fix up a church. They have read of numerous officers, apostles, and prophets and pastors, but they could not fit them together. They just took a few officers—as I did with the wheels of my watch—and made it look like a church, with a deacon and an elder, or an elder and a priest. It might seem like a church, but it was useless to accomplish the thing for which the Church of Christ was established, as my watch was useless without its important wheels, each one fitting into the other; for it is said of old that the head could not say to the foot: "I have no need of thee" (See I Cor. 12); but every officer in his place for his purpose, for the work of the ministry, for the perfecting of the Saints.

*****

Men may duplicate the organization of this Church and when they have done it, when they have fitted in the officers and given them their appointed places, still they shall have a dead thing.

You may establish a perfect system of electric lighting in this building, or in this city, you may have your dynamo, you may have your wires running through the streets, properly insulated, your poles and everything complete, and the globes here, but you can have no light, and no power, until through your perfect system there runs light and power.

And so you may have a perfect church organization, but it will be perfectly dead and useless unless, going through it, there is the power of the living God, which is the source of life and light to this Church.

We have the perfect system and it has radiating through it, the power of the living God, the authority of the Holy Priesthood, and the ordinances thus performed are efficacious and valid for men on the earth and remain sealed upon their heads through their faithfulness, even unto the eternal world.

—Elder Melvin J. Ballard

RESURRECTION

A matron accidentally dropped her gold ring into a glass of acid of some kind. The ring dissolved, and she cried in horror that her ring was gone.

"What happened?" someone asked the now nearly hysterical woman.

"I just dropped my ring into this glass and it all dissolved; it's gone!"

A chemist stepped forward saying, "Oh, no, your ring is not gone. It's still here."

She could not understand that, but he who knew the law of the elements added something to the acid solution and the gold separated, regaining its identity.

The matron took the gold to a goldsmith, and he made a new ring. He had the design and the pattern as he had made it originally, and he made a new ring from the same gold that he had fashioned the old ring.

—Elder Eldred G. Smith

Dr. E. Stanley Jones, a great Protestant missionary and preacher, was in Rome following a
pilgrimage along the routes of the Apostle Paul's
missionary journeys. As a climax he stood at the
opening of the catacombs where lay the remains of
many courageous martyrs of the early Christian
church.

His guide told him, "You can shout in here and
it will echo loudly many times."

"What should I shout?" Dr. Jones wondered.
His mind wandered over the route he had just
traveled, the historic scenes of persecution and
suffering, the scenes of saintly hope and joy in the
message of the Savior, Jesus Christ.

He shouted: "Victory!" And it echoed throughout the catacomb.

———

SACRIFICE

I have heard a great many tell about what they
have suffered for Christ's sake. I am happy to say I
never had occasion to. I have enjoyed a great deal;
but so far as suffering goes I have compared it a
great many times, in my feelings and before
congregations, to a man wearing an old, worn-out,

tattered and dirty coat, and somebody comes
along and gives him one that is new, whole, and
beautiful. This is the comparison I draw when I
think of what I have suffered for the Gospel's
sake—I have thrown away an old coat and have put
on a new one. No man or woman ever heard me
tell about suffering.

"Did you not leave a handsome property in
Ohio, Missouri, and Illinois?" Yes. "And have you
not suffered through that?" No. I have been
growing better and better all the time, and so have
this people. And you may take the history of the
world from the days of Adam down and I am at
the defiance of any historian to prove that the
Saints have suffered as much as the sinners. This is
my belief about the religion of Jesus Christ.

—President Brigham Young

As the great California gold rush began to wane,
Elder Orson Hyde told an April 1854 general
conference congregation in Salt Lake City:

"A great many are now afraid that the gold of
California will all be gone before they get any of
it. Suppose they get it all—suppose they actually
rob the mines of every farthing's worth of value,
what are they going to do with it? Can they place

it beyond the jurisdiction of the Almighty? or put it somewhere where he cannot find it, and use it in a way that he cannot control it? I tell you they may dig, and get all the gold they possibly can, and put it in this bank, or in that; but God will control it all by-and-by, and give it to whom he will; and I will tell you to whom he will give it.

"Says the Apostle to the Corinthians, 'All things are yours, whether Paul, or Apollos, or Cephas, or the world, or life, or death, or things present, or things to come; all are yours, and ye are Christ's, and Christ is God's.' "

SALESMANSHIP

A man strode into a candy store to see customers standing in line to be waited on by one salesgirl while two other salesgirls stood idly by with no customers at all.

The man was interested, so he stood in line waiting for his chance to make a purchase from the busy salesgirl.

"Why?" he asked, "are you so busy and the other girls are not?"

"Oh," she smiled, "as you can see, this store's specialty is bulk candy—usually by the pound. Those other girls fill the scoop and put it on the scales, and then take some of the candy away to make the proper weight. I only fill the scoop to the point to where I have to add a little more candy when my customers' purchases are on the scales."

———————

It is easy to drive a wholesome truth so hard that its usefulness is gone. We are seeking to show a friend some truth that he is missing; we talk patiently with him until it is evident that he sees the truth and is ready to act on it. That is the time for us to drop the matter, and show our confidence in his right spirit and good sense.

But no, we are not satisfied to leave it there; we hang on just a few minutes longer to make sure that he understands, and that he commits himself inescapably to our position; and in that last moment or two we drive him beyond his endurance, antagonize, repel, and make it well-nigh impossible for him to do what he would easily have done had we only stopped short of that last unbearable driving. Going too far we have undone all the good that we had done.

———————

SIN

One summer, part of a backyard was untended, and it soon was taken over by weeds. Belatedly the owner decided to do something about it. At least once a week he pulled the tall weeds out of the patch and stacked them neatly in a nearby compost area. But the man wasn't doing the task that he knew that he should be doing. In pulling out the large, tall weeds he only gave a chance for the other weeds, the ones he never bothered with—to grow and grow more profusely. And so he ended the season with a wonderful crop of weed vines, morning glories and puncture weeds, and the like.

And he mused that so it was with repentance. Repentance to be most effective must be as complete as humanly possible. Just turning from the large sins, like pulling the large weeds, sometimes gives the small sins an excellent chance to flourish.

———————

A man dressed as a devil was walking to a masquerade party when he encountered a pack of dogs. He fled into a church for safety. His unexpected appearance at a church meeting caused panic, and one woman who could not escape with the others plead: "Please, Mr. Devil, I've been a

member of this church for years, but all the time
I've really been on your side."

SPEECH

A local politician was once enmeshed in his
own oratory. Said he:

"Build a chain-link fence around the winter's
supply of summer weather; skim the clouds from
the sky with a teaspoon; catch a thundercloud in a
saucepan; break a hurricane to harness; quiet and
soothe an earthquake; lasso an avalanche; pin a
napkin on the crater of an active volcano—but
never expect to see me false to my principles."

Once, at Wotton, Rowland Hill, the British
postal reformer of the nineteenth century, was
preaching in the afternoon, the only time when it
seemed possible to be drowsy under him. He saw
some sleeping, and paused, saying, "I have heard
that the miller can sleep when the mill is running,
but if it stops it awakens him. I'll try this
method."

And so he sat down, and soon saw an aroused
audience.

SUCCESS

To laugh often and much; to win the respect of intelligent people and the affection of children; to earn the appreciation of honest critics and endure the betrayal of false friends; to appreciate beauty, to find the best in others; to leave the world a bit better, whether by a healthy child, a garden patch, or a redeemed social condition; to know even one life has breathed easier because you lived. This is to have succeeded.

—Ralph Waldo Emerson

———————

The late Alfred P. Sloan, Jr., long-time executive of General Motors Corporation, had a five-point "secret of success." It was:

1. Get the facts.

2. Recognize the equities of all concerned.

3. Realize the necessity of doing a better job every day.

4. Keep an open mind.

5. Work hard.

———————

Success in any calling is the result of a person's love of and belief in the work he has undertaken. Earnest and conscientous labor often accomplishes more in the end than brilliant genius.

TEACHING

In the southern part of Utah there lived a poor widow and her son, the latter a wild, impudent, intractable youth, whose transgressions often brought his mother into sore distress. He was known as the terror of the town. He had almost reached the period of manhood without having curbed this insubordination. One evening the bishopric of the ward in which he lived proposed to him that he attend the Brigham Young Academy. In this proposition they had two purposes; one was that they might rid themselves of him, and the other that he might improve himself. They were willing to furnish the money if he would but go.

When the proposition was placed before him he accepted; his mother agreed to it; and in a very short time he was enrolled as a student in the school. One glance was sufficient to convince his associates that he was not to be trifled with. He came to school with his books under his arm and a six-shooter in his hip pocket. It was difficult for him to accustom himself to his new surroundings; he felt like a young bronco, newly saddled.

Before the end of the first week he had a difficulty with his teacher, to whom he manifested such a degree of insubordination that his instructor appealed to President Karl G. Maeser of the Academy to have him suspended. With bowed head the Principal listened, without uttering a word. Finally he broke the silence and said: "Try him once more; he is the son of a widow, whose entire hope is centered in him. She knows her boy better than we do. She hopes and prays that some day he will see the foolishness of his ways and change them. She has written me several letters in which she has pleaded with me to try to save him. I have promised that I would do my best and I will keep my promise. Give him one more chance."

The instructors returned to their classrooms in compliance with the Master's wishes. Try as they would, all their efforts were in vain, and the young man remained wholly uncontrollable. At the end of another week the instructors returned to the office of the Principal and placed two propositions before him. The one was that this young man should be dismissed from the school forthwith; the other was that in the event the principal could not see his way clear to dismiss him, they would hand in their resignations to take effect immediately. "That young man is a terror," said one of the instructors, "we have done our best, but have failed absolutely."

"Send him to me," said Brother Maeser.

In a very few minutes the young man entered the Principal's office. "Did you send for me?" he asked in a low but defiant voice.

"Yes, sir," replied the genial Principal. "I sent for you because I have to inform you that you must leave this institution tomorrow morning."

"Good," answered the yet unsubdued youth; he then turned about and left the room.

In the middle of the night Brother Maeser awoke from his slumber and thought of the wild youth whom no one seemed able to tame, who was to be expelled from the school the following morning. He thought of the anxious widow and how she had pleaded with him that he might save her son. He arose from his bed, knelt by the side of it and laid the matter before the Lord; saying: "Dear Father, there is at this time a young man in our school whom we are unable to control. We have tried to do our best, but, sad to say, we have failed. If there is a way whereby we may reach him, I pray thee in our Redeemer's name to make it known unto us; and thy name shall have the praise, the honor, and the glory."

Said Dr. Maeser, "I received no satisfaction from my supplication and therefore thought it possible that the Lord himself had given up."

The next morning, about ten o'clock, as the Principal was sitting in his office, there came a knock at the door. Following his call, "Come in," the "black sheep" of the flock entered the room.

"What can I do for you?" asked the Principal. The young man, with downcast eyes, replied: "May I speak with you for a few moments, Professor Maeser?"

"Certainly."

The young man's lips quivered, and with trembling voice, he said: "You will not dismiss me, Brother Maeser, will you? Will you not please give me one more chance?"

Brother Maeser sprang to his feet, extended his arms toward this once obstinate youth and exclaimed: "God bless you, my son! I will not give you up; not one chance but a thousand chances shall we be glad to give you."

The master and the student fell into each other's arms and wept.

This was the turning point in the life of this young man. He studied energetically and worked so industriously that upon various occasions the Principal had to caution him against over-exertion.

You ask, "Whatever became of the boy?" The last we heard of him [and this was written in 1927 at the twenty-sixth anniversary of Dr. Maeser's death] he was a counselor to the bishop who had sent him to Provo to school partly that the ward might be relieved of his presence.

As Dr. James E. Talmage said of Dr. Maeser, "He needs no material monument to perpetuate his memory. The record of his deeds is inscribed in the hearts of his pupils [and their families after them]."

———

The instructor began the discussion in a new teacher-trainer class with: "Don't be merely a vessel to receive; be also a spring to give forth living waters."

———

TEMPLES

The Lord has not offered us these blessings that we might receive them just before we die or when we are old or crippled. What are these blessings for? Not only for eternity, but to be a guide to us and a protection through the struggle of life.

Do you understand why our missionaries go to the temple before they are set apart for the mission fields? This is a requirement of them whether they are eighteen years of age, or twenty, or older, because the Lord has said it should be done. He called all the missionaries to Kirtland in the early days of the Church to receive endowments in the temple erected there. He said this was so that they could go out with greater power from on high and with greater protection.

The endowment received now is greater than that given in Kirtland, for the Lord has revealed additional covenants and obligations for us to keep. If we go into the temple we covenant that we will serve the Lord and observe his commandments. If we realize what we are doing then the endowment will be a protection to us all our lives—a protection which those who do not go to the temple do not have.

—President Joseph Fielding Smith

TEMPTATION

The Sandwich Islander of old believed that the strength and valor of the enemy he killed passed into himself. That may sound ridiculous, but in a way, it is just so with us; we surely gain strength from resisted temptation.

————

Temptations hurt not, though they have access;
Satan o'ercomes none but by willingness.

—Robert Herrick

————

TESTIMONY

It is said that the husbandman is the first to partake of the fruit of the garden and the field, and he then administers it to others; and I want to know if you think you can administer that which you have not got? Now, I can assure you, there is a great deal in these things for you and me to understand; and if we will apply our minds, we shall learn many important lessons. I want to know if you ever heard anything from the Prophets of God about driving people into heaven. Did they ever teach you a doctrine of this kind? No: but it is, "Come, *come,*" all the day long.

—Elder John Young

On a quiet Sabbath afternoon in late fall we stood by the side of the street watching neighbors drive off to Sacrament meeting. There was a huge autumn leaf in the road.

Every automobile that sped created some sort of suction, and for a brief moment that leaf was gaily and happily pulled along toward the goal of the church. That only happened for an instant, then the leaf dropped again to the roadbed motionless to await the coming of another car. Sometimes the next car came in the opposite direction and the leaf followed that car for a brief moment in the way just opposite from the forward motion it had enjoyed moments before.

As our friend drove up to take us to another church assignment at that hour we looked at the leaf for the last time. And somehow we understood how, like that leaf, some people's membership and activity are carried only by the briefest of winds. They seem not to have the great power of testimony to move toward the cherished goal in and of themselves.

———————

THANKSGIVING

If one should give a neighbor a dish of sand and tell him there were particles of iron in it, he might feel for them with his finger in vain. But let the neighbor take a magnet and sweep through the sand, and the iron would be attracted to that magnet—particles, invisible to the eye a moment before, would be gathered by the magnet.

The unthankful heart, like a finger in the sand, discovers no mercies. But let the thankful heart sweep through the day, and as the magnet finds the iron, so finds it every moment some blessings—only the iron in God's sand is more precious than anything on the earth.

———————

So once in every year we throng
    Upon a day apart,
To praise the Lord with feast and song
    In thankfulness of heart.

—Arthur Gutterman

———————

TIME

Time past is gone, thou canst not it recall;
Time is thou hast, improve that portion small;
Time future is not, and may never be.
Time present is the only time for thee.

—Anonymous

———

When time, who steals our years away,
   Shall steal our pleasures too,
The memory of the past will stay
   And half its joys renew.

—Tom Moore

———

TITHING

Tithing is an opportunity, and it is given to us
as such. It is not a "bill" in the sense of our
accounts with business houses. Tithing is an
opportunity whereby we may become partners
with God in the building of his kingdom.

Of course, God is omnipotent. And of course
we are at his mercy. But he has given us our free
agency. We can pay or not, as we like, and whether
we pay or not, the Church will go on prospering

and extending itself throughout the world. The Lord will see to that.

But if we don't pay, the Church may go on without us!

If we fail to help build the kingdom, can we say we are truly a part of it?

If our interest turns to the affairs of this world, can we say we are not *of* the world?

Can any one of us afford to withdraw support from the Lord, especially when each of us is so much in need of his help?

He has made us a great promise: If we pay our tithes and offerings in the true spirit which the Lord intends, he will open the windows of heaven and pour out such blessings upon us that we can hardly contain them.

If we fail to pay, can we be sure of any such favor?

There is a law upon which all blessings are predicated. We obtain the blessing only as we obey the law. Can we afford to miss this opportunity?

—Elder Mark E. Petersen

WORD OF WISDOM

"Bottles and rags! Bottles and rags!" called the ragman, as he plied his calling.

"Why do you always put these words together?" asked a passerby.

"Because, madam," said the ragman, courteously touching his hat to the lady, "whenever you find bottles you find rags."

———

The Lord has told us that "strong drink . . . is not good." Who is it that will say they are when the Lord says they are not?

That man who says "I can drink wine or strong drink, and it not hurt me," is not wise. But some will say, "I know that it did me good, for I was fatigued, and feeble, on a certain occasion, and it revived me, and I was invigorated thereby, and that is sufficient proof for me."

It may be for you, but it would not be for a wise man, for every spirit of this kind will only produce a greater languor when its effects cease to operate upon the human body.

But you know that you are benefited, yes, so does the man who has mortgaged his property know that he is relieved from his present embarrassments; but his temporary relief only binds the chords of bondage more severely around him.

—Patriarch Hyrum Smith
Nauvoo, Illinois
May 28, 1842

WORK

So you think working conditions are bad today? Before you answer, here are some rules that are said to have been posted by a New York company in October 1863:

1.   Office employees each day will fill lamps, clean chimneys, and trim wicks. Wash windows once per week.

2.   Each clerk will bring a bucket of water and a scuttle of coal for the day's business.

3.   Make your pens carefully. You may whittle nibs to your individual taste.

4.   Men employees will be given an evening off each week for courting, or two evenings a week if they go regularly to church.

5. After 13 hours' labor in the office, the employee should spend the remaining time reading the Bible and other good books.

6. An employee who smokes cigars, uses liquor in any form, or frequents pool rooms or public halls, or gets shaved in a barber shop, will be giving good reason to suspect his worth, intentions, integrity, and honesty.

7. The employee who has performed his labors faithfully and without fault for five years will be given an increase of five cents per day in his pay, provided profits from business will permit it.

———————

"Who made you?" a boy of ten was asked.

He stood in thoughtful silence for a moment and then, measuring the length of a baby with his hands, replied: "God made me this long, and I growed the rest."

The mistake that was his in leaving out God in his growth suggests the truth that we are partly self-made men. God and parenthood and birthplace partly make us, but we must make the rest by will and work.

—Wilbur F. Crafts

———————

There is no excellence anywhere without labor. We would think a man foolish indeed who would say, "I am willing that my business should prosper, or that my farm should yield plentifully, but I'll not stir a peg." But he is no more foolish than the man who says, "I am willing that God should bless me abundantly, but I shall not do anything toward that end myself." The missionary or member must consistently rely upon the help of the Lord, but they will not make any progress or meet with any success unless they put forth an earnest effort.

—President Charles W. Nibley

———

When we work to buy enough food to go to work, at that moment—and until our attitude is changed—we are in trouble.

———

YOUTH

"A man has invented a chair that can be adjusted to eight hundred different positions. It is designed for a boy to sit in when he goes to church."

When were those two sentences written? Frankly we don't know. We picked them up in a church publication dated December 1882. It sounds as if that particular problem has been with us a very long time. Let's do everything within our power to keep the youth and the church together always.

———————

In counseling John H. Vandenberg as the new Presiding Bishop of the Church, President David O. McKay said:

"The spirituality of a ward will be commensurate with the activity of the youth in that ward . . . for they will mold the moral atmosphere of the ward."

———————

To you, Youth of today, your fathers bequeath all they have gained without your paying any price to them. But this does not mean that you may sieze all this and make it your own without labor. God has ordained in his infinite wisdom that while man may pass to those who follow him, without price paid to him by them, the things of this earth—the things which moth and rust corrupt and thieves break in and steal—yet man may not freely bequeath (though he may make record thereof) the things of the mind and of the spirit, to be taken without labor by those whom he would favor. Under God's plan every man shall have of the things of the mind and of the spirit those only

which he shall himself conquer. We may quarrel
with this law; we may whine about it, but we
cannot overturn it, for it is founded on infinite
wisdom. It is as fixed as eternity itself.

All men face this law and have had to face it
since the beginning, and Youth would be foolish,
indeed, to allow anything to blind its view of this
truth. Youth must not let self-pity crush their
courage, or drown their industry, or blot out hope.

The world holds for Youth every job it held for
their fathers and all those which their fathers have
added by their conquests of the unknown. Every
step forward in science adds a new job. Youth, do
not allow anyone to make you believe the chaos-
making falsehood that modern invention has made
the world poorer and man less happy. Before you
believe that falsehood, measure in your mind the
life you lead against that led by your grandfather.
Make your mind clear about each thing you have
that you are willing to give up for what he had.

[This radio address was given on KMBC, Kansas
City, Missouri, March 29, 1936. We smile at his
comparisons, being able to add many that were
not known in 1936.]

Will it be your railroads, paved roads, and
automobiles, for his dirt roads, horses and saddles,

and lumber wagons? Will it be your "movie" for his occasional theater, good or bad, or your modern daily newspaper with its illustrations and news from the remote corners of the earth, for his weekly sheet, barren of all yours possesses? Will it be your radio for his profound silence; your bathroom for his wash tub; your warm house for his icy one, except the kitchen; your winter fruits from tropic climes for his wilted apples from the cellar; your varied canned fruits and vegetables for his dried corn and pumpkin; your silk hose for his cotton or woolen socks; your fine comfortable underwear for his red flannel shirts? your easy shoes for his boots made by the corner cobbler?

Consider all these, for all are involved in this much-touted casting away of our machine age. And we have not mentioned the great cultural things which modern invention and machines have brought us.

May I urge Youth to be practical? If any have self-pity, throw it away. Self-pity is the canker that will destroy character.

Look for work, not finding it at once, try again. This was the course your fathers took. Not finding what you would like, take what you can get; so did your fathers. A thousand jobs are open to you which did not exist when your father was young.

This world holds infinitely more for you than it did for your fathers.

Arise, singing, in the early morning and rejoice with the birds; spread out your wings of hope to the rising sun of a new and better day; twitter not to bed with folded wings in the fading glow of a dying day. The world—a greater world than your fathers knew—is yours. But you must overtake and seize it with hands of iron, and grip it that it shall not slip from you, for it will never thrust itself upon you, nor lie idly and limply in your hands once it has been caught.

Ye shall seek, then find, then know the truth, and the truth shall make you free.

—President J. Reuben Clark, Jr.

———

I love the memory of President Wilford Woodruff. There is one thing he went to the Lord for in behalf of the Mutuals of the Church, for which the youth of this people should hold him in high reverence forever and ever, and I will relate it.

There was a time when, through the slackness, through the carelessness of the youth of this people, that their fathers had great concern as to

whether they would qualify to succeed them in
bearing off the responsibility of this work in
maintaining the testimony that the early apostles
and pioneers, that the founders of the Church, had
established; and sometimes this apprehension
would be heard in the congregations of Israel; men
of the older time would rise and express a fear that
when they should pass away the work might
suffer.

President Woodruff, to a certain degree, not
very fully, shared this apprehension. He went into
the woods upon a certain occasion and prayed to
God and asked him concerning the condition of
the youth of his people, and God revealed to him
that: "I have those already among the youth of
my people who will maintain this work and bear
off the responsibility of it forever. Concern thyself
no more."

President Woodruff told me that personally,
and I heard him declare it in effect before public
congregations.

–Elder Junius F. Wells
October General Conference, 1917

———

There was a generation gap between Lucifer
and his Father, but another Son understood
deeper principles and carried on his Father's work.

———